Eric Hughes, Ed.D. University of Washington, is Assistant Professor of Physical Education and Gymnastic Coach at that University. He has been Chairman of the Pacific Northwest Amateur Athletic Union Gymnastic Committee, Vice President of the National Association of Gymnastic Coaches, and Coach of the U. S. National Team that toured Russia, Poland, and Czechoslovakia in 1961.

CONTRIBUTORS

ERIC HUGHES, University of Washington

DOROTHY MacLEAN, University of Washington

BETTY JEAN MAYCOCK, Olympic Competitor
from Kent, Ohio

MARY SARVER, Highline College, Seattle

GEORGE LEWIS, Seattle Y.M.C.A.

GYMNASTICS
FOR GIRLS

A Competitive Approach
for Teacher and Coach

Edited by

ERIC HUGHES
UNIVERSITY OF WASHINGTON

THE RONALD PRESS COMPANY • NEW YORK

Library of Congress Catalog Card Number: 63–19748

Preface

Whenever girls' gymnastics has been introduced into the program as a competitive sport similar to the other physical education activities it has proved to be exceptionally popular. Instead of presenting stunts individually, as in the past, this book offers every stunt as part of a routine. The teaching techniques included show how the individual stunts that are taught will eventually become part of a planned gymnastic composition. Teaching gymnastics in this way is more meaningful to students and much more interesting. For this reason this book stresses official rules and the teaching of competitive routines. These routines, designed to be used from the elementary grades through college, range from a very elementary one to a very difficult one for each event.

The chapter on floor exercises is by Betty Jean Maycock, that on balance beam is by Mary Sarver, and that on vaulting is by Dorothy MacLean. All the other chapters are by Eric Hughes except the one on uneven parallel bars, which was written jointly by Eric Hughes and George Lewis.

A book such as this could not be written without the help of many individuals. Special thanks are due to: Charlie Denny, Richard Hughes, Pete Steilberg, and Jean Hughes for assistance in the preparation of the manuscript; Dale McClements and Jerry Hardy for technical advice; Joyce Tanac, Dale McClements, and Valerie Young for long hours spent in demonstrating stunts; Jim Fraser for photography, and Ione Nelson for illustrations.

ERIC HUGHES

Seattle, Washington
November, 1963

Contents

v

Contents

GYMNASTICS
FOR GIRLS

1

Introduction

PURPOSE OF THE BOOK

The main purpose of this book is to stress that gymnastics is a competitive sport and should be taught as a competitive sport by the physical education teacher as well as by the coach.

Our American way of life is competitive. Adults compete in business, in politics, for offices in civic clubs, and for jobs. Students compete with each other for academic grades, for student offices, for roles in plays, and in music, art, and debate contests. To get more to the point, most activities taught in our physical education program are also of a competitive nature. All the more common sports, whether team, dual, or individual, involve some form of competition. In volleyball and softball teams play against each other and scores are kept. In tennis and badminton individual players compete. In golf and archery scores are kept, and this score is compared with a previous score or with scores made by others. In track and field and swimming, races are held between class members.

During a teaching unit of every sport except gymnastics, the student competes on a team or against another individual many times during the unit. Furthermore, in most activities, "playing the game" is a part of almost every class period. Of course physical educators teach skills and use lead-up drills in these other activities but they do not devote the whole unit, or seldom even an entire class period, to the teaching of these things. To maintain high-level interest, students are encouraged to play the game and compete against other members of the class. In many cases, because of the interest factor, a class is permitted to play the game even though it is not really ready for a competitive game situation.

For almost every activity in our physical education program there is a standard set of rules available. Physical educators believe it is desirable to use standard rules and to use standard equipment (balls of a certain size, nets of a certain height, courts of regulation size). Of course these rules are sometimes modified for inexperienced students or for younger children, but generally teachers follow the rule book and emphasize the importance of the rules. But this is not done in gymnastics. Very few teachers teach this sport according to the rules. In fact many are unaware that there are rules for gymnastics and that specific events are included in the sport. Many teachers who keep up to date in other activities and adopt rule changes immediately are years behind the times in gymnastics. For example, the uneven parallel bars replaced the men's style of parallel bars over ten years ago and yet many women are still teaching the old event.

Why then do teachers who teach every other sport as a competitive activity with standard rules forget about competition and rules when they come to their gymnastics (or tumbling) unit and devote the entire unit to the teaching of individual skills or stunts? The only common technique of a competitive nature used in gymnastic teaching in our schools today is the stunt checkoff list. This enables the individual to compete indirectly against other members of the class. It is a good technique but it is not enough. No wonder gymnastics is not so popular as other sports in our schools.

Competition, of course, is not the only answer to successful gymnastic teaching. A gymnastic unit, or for that matter any other unit, is not likely to be successful unless the teacher organizes the unit and daily lessons thoroughly and teaches with enthusiasm.

This book is designed as a guide for the girls' team coach as well as for the physical education teacher who wants to pep up her instructional program by making it competitive. It is hoped that teachers will be stimulated to start a competitive team in their school. There are many benefits to be derived from participation on a team in modern girls gymnastics designed to include elements of skill, grace, and rhythm rather than strength. The rules safeguard the health of the girl in every possible way. Gymnastics is an excellent competitive activity for girls at the intramural or interschool level.

This idea of competition is consistent with the standards and principles of the Division for Girls and Women's Sports of the American Association for Health, Physical Education and Recreation. This organization was established to promote competition for girls but at the same time to safeguard the participant. Their leaders believe that the value of competition comes, not from what is played, but the way it is played. They believe teachers should stress such things as: enjoyment of the sport, social values, group loyalty, and sportsmanship; and minimize individual achievement and winning of championships.

D.G.W.S. believes participation in sports competition is the privilege of all girls and women.[1] In most schools this objective can best be accomplished by an intramural program. If facilities are available, however, the interschool program should be added to supplement the intraschool program. The D.G.W.S. Standards state: "There is nothing in the creed of education through sports which rules out the expert. There is no defensible reason why an educationally designed sports program should either fear or fail to develop the maximum skill which an individual may possess."[2] Whatever forms, or levels of competition, are sponsored by the school they should be administered according to sound educational principles, and so the greatest number of desirable outcomes result.

The United States is a little behind some other countries in international women's competition. Unless we provide team competition for our girls at the high school level we will continue to take a back seat to other more interested and progressive countries that do have well-organized competition for their young people. Developing female gymnasts of Olympic caliber is not an important objective of a competitive gymnastic program in our schools, but it is an objective that should be given some thought. Americans have dominated most international sport competitions in the past but in recent years have been beaten quite consistently in some sports by the Russians and by other smaller nations. This has hurt our cause considerably in our cold war struggle for world leadership. Every American citizen, especially physical education teachers, should be concerned about this situation.

CHAPTER ORGANIZATION AND CONTENT

Each of the six gymnastic events is dealt with in a separate chapter in this book. For each event, except vaulting, the stunts described are described as part of a routine or exercise (see definitions). There are five routines for each event. Number one in each case is very simple. The skills included can be learned by students of just average ability in just a few class periods. Routine number

---

[1] *Standards in Sports for Girls and Women* (Washington, D.C.: American Association for Health, Physical Education and Recreation, 1953), p. 46.
[2] *Ibid.*, p. 24.

two in each chapter is composed of a combination of beginning and intermediate skills. Number three includes quite a few intermediate skills that are considerably more difficult than those in the first two routines and might be too difficult to present to all students in a physical education class. This routine would be a presentable one for a girl to use in her first year of gymnastic competition. The fourth routine in each chapter includes many advanced skills that would provide a real challenge for the better students in a physical education class. This routine is one that might be used by a competitive gymnast of average ability. Number five is designed for the advanced performer competing on a high school or college team. It is not a routine that could be used in a class situation even for the most advanced students. This routine is the type and caliber that would be used in senior competition in most district meets. It is not as difficult as those used by National champions or Olympic competitors but girls who can master the last routine in any chapter can certainly be classed as excellent performers in that event.

METHOD OF TEACHING ROUTINES

A suggested method of presenting these routines to a class is as follows:

1. *Demonstrate the entire routine.* If the teacher is unable to demonstrate herself, the routine should be taught to a skillful student ahead of time so that she can demonstrate it for the class. If this technique is used, class members can see how the stunts flow together and form a mental picture of the entire routine. This establishes a goal for which they can strive.

2. *Present each stunt separately.* Each stunt should be demonstrated and explained separately. Several stunts can be taught on the same day. The stunts don't have to be taught in the order in which they appear in the routine. The easy ones can be presented first and the harder ones saved until the end.

3. *Divide the routine into parts for practice.* These parts should be made up of three to five stunts. A routine of ten stunts might be divided into parts as follows: Part 1—Stunt 1, 2, 3, and 4; Part 2—Stunt 4, 5, 6, and 7; and Part 3—Stunt 7, 8, 9, and 10. The overlapping of the parts is important. If routines are divided in this way, each stunt can be practiced in the way it must be performed in the full-length routine, that is, immediately following the previous stunt.

4. *Practice the entire routine.* After each stunt has been learned,

and the parts of the routine practiced until they can be reasonably well performed, students should spend a good part of their time performing the routine as a whole. When this stage is reached, another demonstration of the entire routine by an expert performer is a good technique to use.

CLASS ORGANIZATION

It is not one of the purposes of this text to provide detailed information about class organization. Just a few suggestions will be made.

The easiest type of class to teach is one in which the entire class performs the same activity. If the girls have absolutely no background in gymnastics, it is very desirable to introduce one event at a time and have the entire class spend a day or two on this event. This is not always possible because of lack of equipment, but with a little thought and planning, it is possible to keep a large class busy in either tumbling, floor exercise, or balance beam.

Tumbling is a good event to present first. An entire class can be kept busy on just a few mats. Many stunts can be taught across the mats. Other stunts can be executed easily on one mat so an entire squad can work successfully with each member taking her turn on a single mat.

Floor exercises is an activity in which a very large group can participate at the same time. This event requires considerable floor space but absolutely no equipment except possibly a few mats on which some stunts can be learned before being transferred to the bare floor.

The balance beam is also an easy event to organize so that an entire class can work at the same time. Most schools are not equipped with more than one balance beam and only one or two girls can work efficiently on one beam. Some schools might have both a high beam and a low beam. If this is the case twice the number of girls can be kept active. Many girls can be kept busy, though, by using a little initiative and improvising balance beams. Makeshift low beams can be constructed easily and inexpensively in the form of an elongated saw horse about a foot high. Another way to improvise is to lay an ordinary two-by-four on a mat and use this as a balance beam. Girls can practice many balance beam stunts on a line on the floor; in fact many stunts have to be learned on the floor for safety reasons. The first day the balance beam is presented to a class there is no need to use equipment. Lines on the floor, or boards in the floor itself, will serve as beams. In this way every girl in the class can have her own balance beam (line or board) and be active most of the period. In many routines every stunt except the mount and dismount can be practiced on a line on the floor. Even the mount and dismount can be partially learned without utilizing a raised beam.

Vaulting, uneven bars, and trampoline are very difficult events to teach individually to an entire class unless a great deal of equipment is available. The usual way of presenting these three events is to have them all a part of the same class. Tumbling, balance beam, and floor exercises, although they can be presented very successfully alone, can also be included in the same class with the other three events. If this is done there would be six different activities going on in the same class with a different group of girls assigned to each activity. This method of organizing a gymnastic class, called the squad method, is certainly nothing new or different, as many physical education activities are taught in this way.

Teaching a unit in gymnastics to a beginning group might be approached in this way:

1. Teach tumbling to the entire class for one or more class periods.
2. Teach floor exercises to the entire class for one or more class periods.
3. Teach the balance beam event to the entire class for one or more class periods utilizing boards in the floor or lines on the floor rather than equipment.
4. Divide the class into the number of squads desired for the rest of the unit and assign an equal number of squads to each of the three events taught for one or more class periods. Rotate from one event to another during each class period. The low balance beam and the high balance beam can be introduced at this time.
5. Add the trampoline, uneven bars, and vaulting one at a time for the next three class periods in place of one of the tumbling, one of the floor exercises, and one of the balance beam squad stations. If extra equipment is available these events could replace more than one of the other squad stations used for tumbling, floor exercises, or balance beam.

When gymnastic classes are divided into squads it is advisable to keep the squads as small as possible. Three or four to a squad is a good number in considering all factors. For the balance beam and uneven bars the best number to have in a squad is two—one performer and one spotter. For other events it is more desirable to have a few more in each squad. Six to a squad is a maximum for effective teaching. Rather than increase the number in a squad, if the class is large, the teacher should increase the number of squads. Remember students learn by "doing" not by standing and waiting for a turn.

Each squad should have a squad leader who is responsible for the effective functioning of her squad. The partner method of organization can be used very successfully within the squad structure. While one partner performs a stunt or routine, the other partner can spot and offer advice and criticism. *It is very essential in a gymnastic class that spotting techniques be taught to all students as each stunt is taught. Everyone in the class should be a spotter, not just the teacher and squad leaders.*

During each class period squads should be moved or rotated from one event to another. The amount of time spent on each event will vary depending on the age, the physical condition and the ability level of the group. Younger children because of their interest span should be moved more often than older students. Those in poor physical condition have to be rotated rather often. Beginners should be moved more often than advanced performers as they tend to lose interest quickly. For most classroom situations the time spent at one squad station should range from ten to twelve minutes for beginning or younger groups and from twelve to twenty minutes for older or more advanced groups. In schools where the physical education period is very short these suggested time limits should be reduced slightly, however. At a team practice session of one and one half hours in length a group of advanced performers might spend as much as thirty to forty-five minutes on one event. It is not essential that each squad gets practice on each piece of equipment every class period. If a complete rotation can not be made in one class period, squads should be started from the point they ended on the previous day.

Let us assume that we have a class of twenty-four students, who have had some previous gymnastic experience, in a school that is equipped with a side horse, a balance beam, uneven parallel bars, a trampoline, and ample tumbling mats. In this case the class could be divided into six squads of four students and all six events could be included in the same class. If there are more than twenty-four in a class, in this particular school, four students could be assigned to another section of tumbling mats, four could be assigned to another floor exercise practice station, and four could be assigned to practice their balance beam work on a line of the gymnasium floor. A class of thirty-six has now been assigned to nine squads at nine separate squad stations. Four more girls could be assigned to a low horizontal bar, four others to a boys' set of parallel bars with one bar removed if these pieces of equipment are available. Considerable uneven parallel bar work can be taught on a low horizontal bar or on one bar of a boys' set of parallel bars. Forty-four have now been assigned. Let us hope we don't have to be concerned with classes larger than this. Larger classes could be handled, if necessary however, by improvising makeshift balance beams or by assigning squads to other tumbling or floor exercise stations. One can see that a very large class can be taught without necessarily increasing the size of the squads. Every possible piece of equipment should be used before squad size is increased beyond four or five. Even when all equipment is being used, if there is ample floor space for floor exercises and balance beam practice, squad size still need not be increased.

NOMENCLATURE

No attempt has been made to present a complete list of definitions in this text. The more common terms needed for a working knowledge are being defined and are included in a glossary at the end of the book. In some cases terms that apply only to one event will be explained in the chapter devoted to that event. Two very broad and general definitions are appropriate in this chapter.

1. *Gymnastics* (women's) is a competitive sport in which individuals or teams compete by performing routines—either prescribed, optional, or both—in the following six events: floor exercises, side horse vault, balance beam, uneven parallel bars, tumbling, and trampoline. The reason for including this definition is to emphasize that gymnastics is a competitive sport with a definite list of events and specific rules just as are basketball, swimming, and tennis. In the past the term gymnastics was used to refer to all the activities performed in a gymnasium. More recently it was used to refer to a group of activities such as formal calisthenics, Indian club swinging, and wand drills as well as the heavy apparatus activities. These old definitions should give way to the modern one above.

2. *Tumbling* is one of six gymnastic events. This is not meant to be a complete definition. The conduct of the event and the type of stunts used will be explained in the chapter on tumbling. The purpose of including a partial definition at this time is to clarify that "tumbling" and "gymnastics" are not synonymous terms. Many teachers name their unit a "tumbling and gymnastic" unit. The use of tumbling in this manner is not necessary. Some instructors teach tumbling instead of a gymnastic unit. In this case it should be called a tumbling unit.

SAFETY PROCEDURES AND DEVICES

1. Inspect equipment regularly. Check bars for cracks and bolts for tightness. Be sure to have overhead fittings for safety belts and other equipment inspected. It is very important that the bolts holding the wooden rails of the parallel bars in place be loose enough to allow for flexibility of the bar; otherwise the rails will be easily broken.

2. Have enough mats to provide adequate padding. This means double thickness for many stunts. Arrange the mats around the equipment to assure maximum safety. Do not allow mats to overlap so there is a ridge or uneven surface on which to land. Place the mats over the equipment while certain stunts are being learned.

3. Have gymnastic chalk (magnesium carbonate) available to keep the hands dry and thus minimize slipping on the parallel bars, beam, and horse. Chalk or resin is sometimes used on the feet to prevent slipping in tumbling, floor exercise, vaulting, and balance beam.

4. Provide the best possible situation for the activity. Remove hazardous objects. Avoid distractions such as loud yelling at the time difficult stunts are being performed. Keep bouncing balls out of the area. Do not permit horseplay.

5. Lower equipment whenever possible for teaching new stunts in order to minimize the danger from falls, to enable the spotter to work more effectively, and to give the performer confidence.

6. Emphasize spotting. Teach the students how to spot.

7. Have a knowledge of the condition of the students at the start of the activity. Gradually increase the amount of work and the ruggedness of the activity. The instructor or coach should watch for signs of fatigue and stop practice on dangerous stunts when fatigue begins to set in.

8. Make sure students warm up before trying difficult stunts or those that require considerable stretching.

9. Go step by step and make sure students have skill equal to the task. Have students overlearn fundamentals. Follow proper teaching progression. Only present the more difficult stunts to the better students. This means that students probably should be grouped into squads by ability rather than by size, age, or by some other method of classification. Encourage courage but discourage foolish displays of daring. Probably the most important safety precaution is to see that students do not try stunts beyond their ability.

10. Organize and supervise carefully.

EXHIBITIONS

A whole text could be devoted to this subject. Although this book stresses competitive gymnastics, the authors also believe in other related activities and in "show gymnastics." Exhibitions help sell the program and raise the status of the teacher in the school and community. Gymnastics is one of the best activities in our program to use in exhibitions for assemblies, P.T.A. meetings, and other school and community functions. Exhibitions have much the same value as competitions. They help motivate the students participating and also increase interest in the activity among other students in the school. An excellent exhibition can be put on with students of just average ability from a physical education class if the demonstration is planned carefully. If the school administration does not believe in interschool competition for girls, the next best thing to stimulate the better performers is an exhibition team or club. Girls with special ability and interest should be given an opportunity to participate in gymnastics as an extracurricular activity and have the thrill of performing for an audience if they are deprived of the opportunity of team competition. With our present emphasis on physical fitness it seems especially appropriate to offer considerable extracurricular as well as curricular gymnastic activity. Exhibitions are a vital part of the overall gymnastic program.

SELECTION OF GYMNASTIC EQUIPMENT

Until recently, our American gymnastic equipment companies did not produce satisfactory equipment. Several are still producing inferior equipment. One company manufactures one design that is very usable and yet still produces another that is very poor. Competition with excellent European equipment has forced our American companies to come out with new designs and to start producing modern, serviceable apparatus of excellent quality.

Because there is still some very unsatisfactory equipment being produced in this country it is necessary for a purchaser to select equipment carefully. Many schools have purchased poor equipment in recent years because of lack of knowledge on the part of physical education personnel. Insist on equipment that is *easy to move* and *easy to adjust*. Above all, insist on equipment that *meets official specifications*. Physical educators would certainly not purchase tennis balls the size of a softball but would insist on official balls. They would not recommend the purchase of a volleyball net made out of plywood or a soccer ball made out of sponge rubber but would request the purchase of regulation equipment. Few purchasers of gymnastic equipment bother to take the same precautions in selecting items that cost many times the amount of these other more common items.

Good equipment is now available. Make sure you get it.

Many school districts insist on purchasing from the lowest bidder. Sometimes a physical education teacher is prevented from getting the equipment she desires because of this rule, even though she knows the difference that exists in equipment produced. This practice is especially unfortunate in the purchase of gymnastic equipment as it will have to be used for twenty, thirty, or even forty years before being replaced.

This does not mean that all equipment has to be expensive. Homemade equipment can be very usable and satisfactory. A vaulting box is a satisfactory substitute for a side horse until the funds are available for the purchase of a regulation side horse. Balance beams that compare very favorably with any commercially produced beam can be made in a school shop.

START YOUR PROGRAM NOW

If the average physical education teacher waits until she feels fully prepared and qualified to teach gymnastics before introducing it to her program, she will never start the activity. None of us feels completely qualified in this sport. There is so much to learn and such a variety of skills involved that only a few will ever become experts in all phases of the activity. That is what makes it so interesting. There is a challenge for all. Teachers are always learners in this sport, more so than in other activities. They can learn along with their students. They should read as much as possible, attend clinics, and order films occasionally in order to observe what the experts are doing. Gymnastic teachers do not necessarily have to be performers themselves.

Teachers do not have to wait until they have equipment to start gymnastics. It would be nice to start with all the regulation equipment, but remember—tumbling mats are really the only necessary item for a satisfactory program. A little improvising with equipment will enable those with initiative to get a program into low gear. A good unit could be taught including only tumbling, floor exercises, and balance beam work done on lines on the floor and two-by-fours resting on two blocks of wood. Do not be content for long with this minimum equipment program but get out of low gear and into second gear by utilizing a boy's horizontal bar or boys' parallel bars converted to uneven bars and by constructing a box horse or balance beam. The next step is regulation equipment for a high geared program.

Teaching modern girls gymnastics is very satisfying. Start right away; it will be a challenge and a thrill. This sport is different and exciting. It is a very popular activity in most of Europe and the Far East. It can be made popular in this country too. Our girls need this type of activity. A physical education program is not complete unless it includes the sport of gymnastics.

2

Tumbling

Tumbling undoubtedly is the most important of all our gymnastic activities. It can be performed indoors on mats or out-of-doors on the lawn, in the park, or on the beach. It is a natural activity for children. Children make up stunts and try to tumble even though they have never been exposed to the activity. It is an excellent background activity for the other gymnastic events and for other sports. Although tumbling takes more strength than many of our popular sports, it does not take a great amount of strength and so is suitable for almost every girl from kindergarten through college.

Tumbling has many values. It develops the basic physical qualities of agility, flexibility, balance, power, strength, and endurance. Timing and coordination are also developed. A tumbler learns to fall properly and how to control her body. One of the greatest values of this activity is the development of courage and self-confidence in activities where falls, body contact, or any type of unusual movement is involved.

Tumbling is taught as a physical education activity in almost every civilized country in the world. A large class can be taught by one teacher in a relatively small area. As tumblers become more advanced, however, they need a longer row of mats and more running space. Routines in group I, II, and III in this chapter require a row of mats 30 feet long. Routines in group IV and V require 40 to 50 feet of mats. This does not mean that mats need to be placed in 30- or 40-foot sections for every class period. Most of the stunts can be taught on a single 5′ × 10′ mat. Many stunts can be taught with students working across a 5′ × 10′ mat. If this is done, three or four students can work on a single mat.

It is much better to keep the students active on a small mat area than to have them standing in a line waiting for their turn on a long row of mats. Several times during a tumbling unit, or possibly for a short time during every class period, the mats should be placed in 30- or 40-foot sections so that students may perform their entire routines after they have learned the individual stunts in the routines.

Tumbling is one of the most common and popular competitive gymnastic events. This is true throughout the world, even though it is not a competitive event in the Olympics or in other international competition. It is a competitive event for both men and women in the United States and Canada. In Sweden and in many other foreign countries, it is a competitive event for children and young men and women in junior competitions. In Germany they sometimes hold double tumbling (two people) competition.

Tumbling rules for competition are brief and uncomplicated. Rules call for a minimum mat length of 60 feet, a width of 5 feet, and a thickness of 2 to 4 inches. The mats should be tied together and have a firm and nonslippery surface. Collegiate rules for men also call for a single cover mat of at least one inch of thickness 60 feet by 5 feet. When space permits, more than 60 feet of mats is suggested. A performer may utilize more area than is covered by mats by going off the end of the mats to obtain a running start or by tumbling off the end of the mats during one of her series. It is considered poor form, however, and points are deducted by the judges, if she touches the floor on either side of the mat. A competitor may leave the mats to perform certain stunts or routines on the floor if she prefers.

The tumbling event is limited to a maximum of four "trips down the mat" or series of not more than two minutes total duration. (In collegiate competition for men the maximum duration of the tumbling event is one and one-half minutes.) The two-minute time limit includes the rest periods between the trips. Overly long rests, not commensurate with the difficulty of the contestants' routines, are penalized by the judges. So long as the performer begins her run for her last trip before the two minutes are up, she is given credit for the whole trip. Warning times are usually given the competitor during her rest periods at the end of the mat.

One rule that should be emphasized for girls is: "Strictly tumbling routines are to be performed. Contortional or dance movements are not considered to be tumbling routines." [1] Coaches should make sure that their students fully understand and abide by this rule.

Apart from the above quoted rule there is nothing in the rules to give information about what stunts should be included or about

---

[1] *Gymnastics—Official Rules Men and Women* (A.A.U., 1962–63), p. 172.

how the four trips should be composed. This means that a competitor has free reign in selection and composition of her particular routine or exercise. Over a period of years several practices have become generally accepted, however, and should probably be considered by the competitor and coach. Only fast moving stunts are considered as tumbling stunts. Front or back walkovers, for example, are not considered tumbling stunts. (These stunts can be used in the floor exercise event.) Routines should be continuous without stops or pauses. Both front (forward roll, front handspring, front somersault) and back (back roll, back handspring, back somersault) tumbling should be included in the complete competitive exercise. Some say side tumbling (cartwheels and side somersaults) should also be included, but this is not a generally accepted belief. It is general practice to have one or more trips combining forward, backward, or sideward moving stunts. Examples of these are included in all groups of routines in this chapter. Another unwritten rule accepted in most competition, and which the author believes should be adopted officially by the rules committee, is the elimination of the "interrupted" or "double-barreled" trip down the mat. Some competitors perform a short trip and then, finding considerable mat left, take another run and perform another short routine or single stunt as they leave the mat. This should be counted as two trips or penalized as a major break as in other gymnastic events. A trip once started should be continuous. Extra steps in the middle of a routine should always be considered as a break and penalized by the judges.

ABBREVIATED ROUTINE DESCRIPTIONS

   I. A. Forward roll, forward roll, jump half pirouette, backward roll, backward roll
     B. Forward roll with a walkout, cartwheel, cartwheel, forward roll
  II. A. Roundoff, backward roll, backward extension roll, backward roll, backward extension roll
     B. Cartwheel, cartwheel, forward roll walkout, roundoff, backward extension roll
 III. A. Front handspring, forward roll, diving forward roll, forward roll walkout, cartwheel
     B. Roundoff, backward roll, backward extension roll, fishflop, squat through, snap-up
     C. Headspring, forward roll, headspring, forward roll, headspring
 IV. A. Front handspring, headsprings in series

     B. Roundoff, back handspring, backward extension roll, fishflop, squat through, snap-up
     C. Cartwheel, cartwheel, roundoff, back handspring walkout with half turn, handspring, headspring
  V. A. Roundoff, series of back handsprings
     B. Front handspring walkout, front-handspring walkout, roundoff, back-handspring walkout with half turn, front handspring
     C. Front somersault, forward roll, headsprings in series
     D. Roundoff, back handspring, back somersault

Other Advanced Stunts Described
    1. Layout back somersault
    2. Whip-backs in series
    3. Front handspring—front somersault
    4. Full twisting back somersault.

I. BEGINNING ROUTINE IN DETAIL

SERIES A

1. Forward Roll (Fig. 2–1).   From the standing position the performer bends forward at the waist and reaches for the mat with the hands a shoulder width apart (1). The arms actually lower the body to the mat. The chin is placed on the chest and the legs give a little push (2). The back of the head contacts the mat, then the back of the shoulders. As the shoulders make contact with the mat, the hands are taken off the mat and grasp the shins to pull the body and legs into a tight tuck position (3). An alternate method is to reach forward as far as possible on each side of the legs as the hands are taken off the mat. The head and shoulders should be kept forward at this point to aid in rolling to the feet (4).

TEACHING TECHNIQUES. This stunt should be taught from a squat position before being taught from a stand. If a girl has

    1   2   3   4

Fig. 2–1.   Forward roll.

difficulty rolling in a straight line or in getting her head tucked under so she can start to roll, have her straighten her legs somewhat in the squat position, thus raising her hips higher. If she has trouble rolling all the way up to the feet, have her get down on her back on the mat and practice rocking back and forth in the tuck position grasping the shins. Emphasize a tight tuck and a forward lean of the head and shoulders. It is easier to roll to the feet if the knees are together and the feet wide apart with the toes turned out. This is considered poor form but might be suggested to girls who are having considerable trouble.

SPOTTING. Many girls will not need to be spotted for the forward roll but it is wise to be cautious. One hand can be used behind the head to aid in tucking the chin on the chest. The other hand can be placed under the abdomen or in front of the hips to help start the forward motion and to bear some of the tumbler's body weight. The spotter should be down on her knees on the mat close to the performer. Make sure all girls learn how to spot and get practice in spotting. If they learn how to spot the simple stunts, they will then be better able to spot the difficult ones.

2. Forward Roll. The second forward roll in this routine is exactly like the first except that it starts from a squat position instead of from a stand and therefore is easier.

3. Jump Half Pirouette (Fig. 2–2). This is nothing more than a jump in the air with a 180 degree turn so that the tumbler lands facing the opposite direction. As the second forward roll is completed, the legs should be straightened rapidly. A high jump should be encouraged to give "life" to the routine. Reaching with the arms straight above the head will give extra height and probably result in a better half pirouette (1). The head should look in the direc-

Fig. 2–2. Jump half pirouette.

1

tion of the turn but should be kept in an erect position. Looking
down at the mat usually results in landing off-balance.

4. Backward Roll (Fig. 2–3).   Upon landing from the half pirouette, the performer leans backward and bends the knees rapidly (1).
As the point of the buttocks makes contact with the ground, the chin
should be forward on the chest and the hands should reach over
the shoulders with palms up and thumbs toward the ears (2).   The
hands will make quicker and better contact with the mat if the
elbows are kept well forward in front of the body.   The chin should
be kept on the chest and the knees close to the chest throughout
the roll.   As the hands make contact with the mat, the arms push to
help lift the head off the mat.   The roll is completed by straightening the knees slightly and reaching for the mat with the feet (3).
A common mistake is to land on the knees or on the entire lower leg.
This is caused by straightening at the hips rather than at the knees
in completing the roll.

TEACHING TECHNIQUES.   This stunt should be taught first from a
squat position with the hands on the mat well in front of the body.
The first movement should be to rock forward onto the hands before pushing backward onto the buttocks.   A good technique is to
practice reaching over the shoulders while in this squat stand to
make sure the hands are in the right position before attempting the
roll.   Another technique is to lie on the back and rock back and
forth in a tuck position with the knees close to the chest.   The hands
should make contact with the mat over the shoulders each time that
the performer rolls back onto the upper back.   This drill is completed by rolling all the way over to the feet as in the regular backward roll.

SPOTTING.   Spot every girl at first. For heavy girls place a
spotter on each side. Make sure everyone learns the spotting
technique and gets practice in spotting. The spotter should lift
some of the performers weight as the stunt is being learned.   This

1   2   3

Fig. 2–3.   Backward roll.

can be done by standing and reaching over the buttocks of the girl with one hand on each hip or by kneeling beside her and lifting with one hand under the hip or front of the thigh. The spotter should not push on the lower back of the tumbler to help her over as this often results in injury to the neck.

5. Backward Roll. The second backward roll is the same as the first except that it starts in the squat position and therefore is easier.

SERIES B

1. Forward Roll Walkout (Fig. 2–4). A forward roll with a walk-out is started exactly the same as a regular forward roll. The only difference is that at the completion of the roll only one leg is kept tucked while the other is extended forward (1). The weight of the body, therefore, is first placed on the bent leg, and then as this leg is straightened it shifts forward to the other leg (2). The purpose of a walkout forward roll is to permit a more fluid movement into the next stunt of the series when the next stunt is one that is executed with a one-foot takeoff.

1   2

Fig. 2–4.   Forward roll walkout.

2. Cartwheel (Fig. 2–5). As the walkout forward roll is completed, the tumbler will be in a semistanding position with the feet quite wide apart (1). Either foot can be forward, but the description here will be given only with the left foot forward. The left hand is placed in the center of the mat. The head should be kept up (chin off the chest). There should be a push first off the right foot and then off the left foot (2). As the left foot pushes, the right hand reaches for the center of the mat slightly more than shoulder width from the left hand. This first part of the cartwheel actually is a sideward kick into a handstand (3). As the motion continues, the right foot reaches for the center of the mat. This is accomplished by bending at the waist (4). If enough momentum is started on the takeoff, the left foot will follow and can also be placed in the

Fig. 2–5. Cartwheel.

center of the mat a few feet from the right foot so that the performer ends in a standing position facing the side of the mat.

TEACHING TECHNIQUES.   Start teaching the cartwheel facing the side of the mat with the feet quite wide apart and the arms stretched to the side. A rock to the right precedes a cartwheel done to the left. It helps many students to place a tumbling slipper or some other small object on the left side of the mat in a position that will be about equal distance between the hands in their position on the mat as the cartwheel is executed. The eyes should be kept on this object throughout the stunt. If a student has considerable trouble with the cartwheel, have her try it to the other side. This might solve the problem. Draw a chalk line down the center of the mat so that hands and feet can be aimed for this line. Suggest to those who have trouble that the cartwheel be started from a partial squat position and finish in a partial squat position. The legs can gradually be straightened as the performer "gets the feel" of the stunt. A student who has trouble with the finish of the cartwheel should be supported in a handstand. She can drop the right foot from this position close to the right hand and then take a quarter turn to the left and thus "get the feel" of the finish of the stunt.

SPOTTING.   The spotter stands behind the performer and reaches for the performers right hip with her left hand and the left hip with her right hand. The performer can be guided through the cartwheel in this way. At the start of this spotting technique the spotter's arms will be crossed with the left over the right. When the performer is in the handstand position, the arms will be in a normal position. As the cartwheel is completed, the arms will again be crossed with the right over the left.

3. Cartwheel. The second cartwheel is the same as the first except that it starts from a standing position facing the side of the mat.

4. Forward Roll. Following the second cartwheel in this series there is a quarter twist on the right foot as it touches the mat. The movement continues forward on the left foot and the roll is done in the same direction as the rest of the stunts in the series.

II. LOW INTERMEDIATE ROUTINE IN DETAIL

SERIES A

1. Roundoff (Fig. 2–6). The roundoff is one of our most important tumbling stunts as it is used to start most backward moving routines, even at the advanced level. The purpose of the stunt is to change forward run to backward movement. It is very similar to the cartwheel and yet quite different. The roundoff may be done to either side but is only described to the right in this series.

The stunt starts with a run and a hop on the right foot with the left foot raised very slightly forward. The arms should also be raised to about face height. It is important to maintain a forward lean of the body at this time (1). If the arms are raised higher than the face or if the forward leg is raised too high, there is a tendency for a beginner to lean backward. The left foot, or forward foot, is placed on the mat as the body bends forward at the waist and the

1   2   3   4   5

Fig. 2–6. Roundoff.

hands reach for the center of the mat (2). Both hands reach for the mat at the same time; however, the left hand will make contact first. The fingers of the left hand point toward the left side of the mat while the fingers of the right hand point back in the direction of the run. The right hand is placed about a foot from the left hand and either straight ahead or slightly to the left of the left hand. It is very important that the entire body be facing in the direction of the movement until the actual reach for the mat. At this time the upper body will start to twist. It is also important that both hands reach for the center of the mat and not be placed out to the left side of the mat. The right foot is thrown over head followed by the left foot, which pushes vigorously off the mat. The head should remain up—that is, chin off the chest. As the feet pass vertically over the hands and head, the feet come together (3). The body executes a quarter turn during the first part of the roundoff and then another quarter turn as the body is rapidly flexed to snap the feet to the mat (4). At the time the feet are snapped down, there is a vigorous push from the fingers and shoulders. The feet usually make contact with the mat so that they are in front of the center of gravity. The body is, therefore, off-balance backward (5). This is true when a roll or a back handspring follows the roundoff but not when a back somersault is the next stunt.

2. Backward Roll. The backward roll has already been described in Routine I–A.

3. Backward Extension Roll (Fig. 2–7). This stunt is a backward roll to a momentary hand-stand followed by a rapid snap-down to the feet. It should be taught to beginners using the same start as a regular backward roll; however, when it has been learned it is usually started from a stand with a straight leg sit-down. To fall backward from a stand with a straight leg the body should lean sharply forward from the waist. The hands may be placed beside the hips with the fingers pointing toward the toes to catch part of the weight but this is not necessary if the body is leaned well forward (1). As the weight rolls backward and the back of the head contacts the mat, the performer is in a pike position with the legs straight (2). From this position the body is rapidly extended and the feet are pushed toward the ceiling (3). There must be a hard push off the mat with both the hands and the head. Most teachers don't emphasize the head push enough. When the handstand position is reached (4), the feet are snapped toward the mat with a rapid flexing at the hips. At the same time there should be a vigorous push from the shoulders and fingers so that momentarily both the hands and the feet are off the mat (5).

Fig. 2–7. Backward extension roll.

SPOTTING. It helps some students to have the instructor stand beside them as they roll, grasp the near thigh, and help lift the legs to the handstand position. This will aid the student to "get the feel" of the rapid extension.

TEACHING HINTS. The finish of the stunt may be practiced separately by kicking to a momentary handstand and practicing the snap down and the shoulder push from this position.

4 and 5. Backward Roll and Backward Extension Roll. The two stunts that complete this routine have already been described—the backward roll in series I–A and the extension roll immediately above.

SERIES B

Cartwheel, cartwheel, forward roll with a walk out, roundoff, backward extension roll.

The five stunts included in this trip down the mat have been previously described. They are combined in a slightly different way, however, in this series. The first cartwheel should be done from a run with a skip takeoff similar to the roundoff in Routine II–A. The roundoff in this routine is not done with a run but is executed immediately after the forward roll with a walkout.

III. INTERMEDIATE ROUTINE IN DETAIL

SERIES A

1. Handspring (Fig. 2–8). The handspring starts with a run and a skip takeoff the same as that used for the roundoff. The performer

Fig. 2–8.   Handspring.

hops on the right foot, with the left foot raised slightly in front. The arms are raised forward to about face height and the body maintains a forward lean (1). As the hands reach forward for the mat, the left foot makes contact with the ground and the right foot is thrown up over the head. The hands are placed on the mat shoulder width apart about two feet in front of the left foot. The arms should be perfectly straight and the head back (chin off the chest) with the eyes focused on a spot on the mat about a foot in front of the hands (2). About the time the hands make contact with the mat, or maybe slightly before they touch the mat, the left foot thrusts vigorously off the mat and follows the right foot overhead (3). As the legs reach the handstand position, the hands leave the mat and the feet continue their circling arc over to the mat (4, 5, 6). This is described as a push in most texts but is actually more of a rebound off the hands with the push from the fingers and the thrust from the shoulders being secondary in importance. If the approach and first part of the handspring are executed correctly, the hands will remain on the mat only a fraction of a second. The rebounding effect will be lost entirely if the arms are bent or if the shoulders are allowed to get in front of the hands when the hands are on the mat (see Fig. 2–9). At the time of the rebound off the mat the lower arms, upper arms, and trunk should form a straight line with the shoulders extended as far as possible. A performer who gets a good rebound off the hands will be able to complete the handspring in an arched or straight body position on the feet. Beginners will not be able to get enough lift off the hands and will have to bend at the knees on the landing. Even with beginners, however, an arched body landing should be emphasized and practiced, so that a bend

4   5   6

Fig. 2–8. *Continued.*

at the knees and hips does not become a permanent bad habit. In a good handspring the head will be slightly back on the landing and the arms will be above the head.

TEACHING TECHNIQUES. a) Have students practice the approach and kick to the handstand position without going over. A spotter or partner can stand in readiness to catch the back of the thighs as the handstand position is reached and to push the performer back to her feet. This technique teaches the performer to keep the shoulders above the hands and the arms straight. b)Have the girls practice the approach and kick as if to do the handspring but just before the vertical position is reached to rebound off the mat and hop forward a foot or two with the hands. The vertical position is never quite reached and the feet drop back to the mat without completing the

WRONG   RIGHT

Fig. 2–9. Handspring.

handspring. This teaches the rebound off the mat with the hands remaining in contact with the mat for only a fractiion of a second. c) The hands may be placed on a rolled mat to give a little extra height as the handspring is learned. This technique does not always make the handspring easier and sometimes brings about bad habits so should be used cautiously. d) On no condition allow students to place their hands on the floor and arch over a rolled mat. This technique is used by some teachers, but it teaches bad habits such as tucking the head on the chest and staying on the hands too long. e) A common mistake for girls that isn't common with boys is to leave one hand on the mat much longer than the other. To correct this fault the spotter on this side should lift hard under the upper back to make sure that both hands come off the mat at the same time.

Photo by Jim Fraser

Joyce Tanac Performing a Front Handspring with a Walkout. Notice the straight line formed by the upper trunk and arms and that the hands have already left the floor while the shoulders are still over the hands. Joyce is a twelve-year-old Seattle prodigy. She was Pacific Northwest Novice All-Round Champion in 1962.

Spotting. This can be done by placing the performer in a hand belt or by two girls grasping hands or holding a towel under the small of the back of the performer as she executes the handspring. Probably the best method is to have two spotters kneeling one on each side of the spot where the hands will be placed. The spotter's hand nearest the performer as she approaches is placed on the lower arm while the other hand is placed on the upper back. The hand under the back does most of the lifting.

2. Forward Roll. This stunt was described in Routine I–A.

3. Diving Forward Roll (Fig. 2–10). This is done exactly the same as a regular forward roll except there is more of a spring from

1   2

Fig. 2–10. Diving forward roll.

the legs and a forward reach with the hands. The feet actually leave the mat before the hands touch the mat (1). In this position in the air the legs should be straight and together with the toes pointed. The head remains back with the eyes watching the mat as long as possible (2). If the head is tucked too soon, the performer will drop hard onto the upper back and will receive quite a jar.

4 and 5. Forward Roll Walkout and Cartwheel. The last two stunts in this routine were explained in Routine I–B.

SERIES B

1, 2, and 3. Roundoff, Backward Roll, and Backward Extension Roll. The first three stunts in this routine have been described previously in the chapter. The last three stunts are new, however, and are explained below. The reader should note that there are actually three backward rolls in this series. The first is a regular tucked backward roll, the second an extension roll finishing with a snap-down to the feet, and the third an extension roll that ends with a chest roll-down.

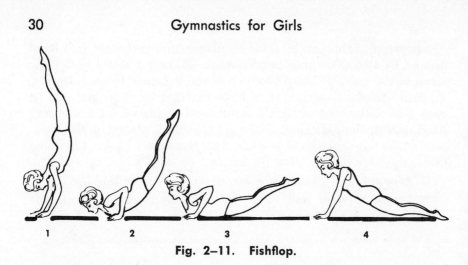

Fig. 2–11. Fishflop.

4. Fishflop (Fig. 2–11). Fishflop is the common name given to a backward extension roll that is completed with a chest roll on the mat instead of with a snap-down to the feet. The first part of the stunt is done exactly the same as the backward extension roll. When the handstand position is reached, the performer quickly bends the arms and lowers the chest to the mat (1, 2). If the body remains in a good arched position, a smooth roll down can be executed from the chest, to the abdomen, to the legs (3). As the chest roll is completed, the upper body will rock up off the mat (4). The arms are straight in this position and support the weight of the upper body.

TEACHING TECHNIQUES. Don't insist that a beginner get all the way to the handstand before lowering the chest to the mat. The stunt can be executed if the arms are straightened just enough to get the head through. In fact, if the head is twisted to the side a little, it can be executed without the head being lifted off the mat. Do not encourage this type of fishflop, however, but instruct the performers to push with the hands and get as high as possible.

SPOTTING. Stand on the side of the performer and as the chest is lowered to the mat reach under the thighs with one arm and lower the performer to the mat. The spotter does not have to grasp the performer in any way. The legs of the performer merely lay across the arm of the spotter during the chest roll.

5. Squat-Through (Fig. 2–12). The squat-through starts from a front leaning rest or boy's push-up position (1). As the chest roll is completed, the performer springs off the lower legs and feet and quickly brings the knees up toward the chest so that the body can pass between the arms in a tucked position (2a). Flexible girls can squat through the arms in this manner to a sitting position on the mat without raising their hands off the mat and without bending their legs. This is called a stoop-through (2b). Other girls, however, will have to give a good push upward with the hands in order to raise the shoulders enough to permit the legs to squat through the arms. The squat- or stoop-through ends in a sitting position on the mat with the legs straight out in front and the trunk vertical (3).

Fig. 2–12.   Squat-through.

6. Snap-Up (Fig. 2–13). This stunt is often called a neck spring or a kip-up. It starts from the sitting position described above (1). The first part of the stunt is similar to a backward roll except the legs are kept perfectly straight. The performer rolls onto the back of the neck and the hands reach over the shoulders to make contact with the mat. The hips should be raised high off the mat with the thighs directly above and close to the face in a tight pike position (2). The tumbler immediately starts to roll or rock back in the opposite direction maintaining the tight pike position with the legs straight (3). This slight roll or rock back is very important. After the hips have moved about six inches, the kipping motion starts. This consists of a rapid extension of the body and a hard push with the hands (4). The legs actually go through a rotary movement—up, out, and then down. They should be straight during this kipping motion. It makes it much easier to get to the feet if the knees are bent on the landing and the feet placed quite far apart with the toes turned out (5a). As the girl gets better, she can try to keep her legs together and straight and come to a stand with an arched back and arms above the head (5b). This second method is considered much better form and should be emphasized in teaching.

TEACHING TECHNIQUES. Do not let students start the snap-up from a lying position on the mat with the hands already in position for the push. It might seem easier from this position, but the rhythm and timing of the stunt is lost if this is permitted.

Some girls find it hard to get the idea of keeping the buttocks off the mat in the snap-up. To correct this the leg motion and landing position can be practiced alone without any arm push and without

Fig. 2–13.   Snap-up.

the head and shoulders leaving the mat. The roll into the pike position, the slight rock back in this position, the body extension with
the rotary leg motion, and the placement of the feet for the landing
can all be practiced in this drill. At the completion of this practice
drill the feet are on the mat, the legs are bent at the knees, and the
body is arched from the knees to the shoulders with the hips in the
air well off the mat.

SPOTTING.   This is a difficult stunt to spot successfully. The spot
is used as an assist in learning the stunt as there is no real need to
spot from a safety standpoint. The spotter kneels beside the tumbler
as she rolls back onto her shoulders and places one hand under her
lower back and one hand under her upper back. An assist can be
given with both hands at the time of the kipping motion.

SERIES C

1. Headspring (Fig. 2–14). The headspring starts with a short
running approach and a two-foot takeoff (1). Do not allow students
to use a one-foot takeoff for a headspring as it changes the entire
technique of the stunt and it becomes more like a handspring with
bent arms than a headspring. The performer leans forward from
the waist and places the hands on the mat about shoulder width
apart. The front part of the head (approximately the hairline not
the forehead) is also placed on the mat slightly in front of the hands.
The tumbler then jumps or pushes from both feet into a pike position with the legs straight and the feet slightly lower than the hips
(2). In this pike position there is a slight fall offbalance before any
leg motion starts. This is a very important part of the headspring
(3). After the center of gravity has moved well beyond the points
of support, the legs whip hard in a rotary movement and the arms
push hard off the mat (4). In this first headspring in the series the

Fig. 2–13. *Continued.*

legs will have to be bent a little on the landing so that the performer can proceed quickly into the next stunt (5). An arched back landing (used in the third headspring of the series) is considered better form, however, and should be emphasized in teaching.

TEACHING TECHNIQUES. Roll a mat loosely so that it will form a flat surface on the top. This rolled mat should be about a foot high. Students place their hands and head on this mat in learning the headspring. The extra height makes it easier to get to the feet. As the performer becomes more proficient, the height of the rolled mat can be reduced gradually until the headspring can be performed on the level mat.

SPOTTING. Two spotters sit facing each other on this rolled mat. The performer places her hands and head on the mat between the spotters. The spotters place one hand on the performer's forearm and one under her upper back. The hand on the forearm protects the spotters from flying arms and also enables the spotters to control the landing. The hand under the upper back does most of the lifting. It is a good technique for the spotters to assist students who are

Fig. 2–14. Headspring.

Photo by Jim Fraser

Spotting for a Slow-Motion Headspring. Notice that in this photo one hand is on the upper back and one is holding the legs in the pike position. As the performer falls off-balance, the hand will shift from the leg to the arm.

having trouble with slow motion headsprings. The hand closest to the performer is placed on the leg, the other under the upper back. The performer can thus be held in a pike position. The fall off-balance can be initiated and controlled by the spotters. At the right point in the fall off-balance, the hand on the leg can initiate the whipping motion of the performers legs and then quickly shift to the performer's forearm.

2. Forward Roll. Previously described in Routine I–A.

3. Headspring. This second headspring in this series is done exactly as the first. It is a little more difficult to do a headspring immediately after a forward roll than it is to do one from a running approach. Because there isn't as much forward motion, there is a tendency for students to start the whipping motion of the legs too soon, before the body has fallen off-balance in the pike position. There is also a tendency to place the hands too close to the feet. This usually results in the head being tucked under too far so that the weight is on the back of the head. As the performer completes the forward roll she should reach well forward with the hands and make sure the front of the head is placed on the mat.

4. Forward Roll. Previously described in Routine I–A.

5. Headspring (with Arched Landing) (Fig. 2–15). This is approximately the same stunt as the previous two headsprings in this series; however, as the tumbler gets better, one change can be made. If the performer whips the legs hard and pushes hard with the hands, it is possible to come to a stand with the feet and legs together and the hips forward so that the landing will be in an arched position with the hands above the head. It is hard to do another stunt im-

Fig. 2–15.   Headspring (with arched landing.)

mediately following a landing in this position, but it is a very good landing to use for the last headspring in a series (1). This type of landing should be emphasized when teaching the headspring. If spotters are used to give an assist during the learning process, most girls can accomplish an arched back landing.

IV.   LOW ADVANCED ROUTINE IN DETAIL

SERIES A

Front Handspring, Headsprings in Series. Although there is only one new stunt in the three series in Routine IV, the combination of stunts is much more difficult and therefore the routines are more advanced. Both stunts in this first series have been explained earlier in the chapter.

Headsprings done one after the other are a little more difficult than done singly as they were in the previous routine. A series of headsprings should be done quite quickly to be impressive, so the

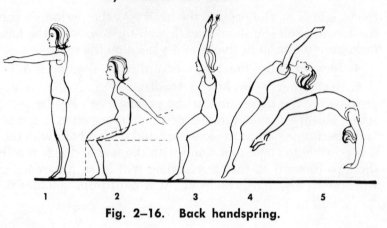

Fig. 2–16. Back handspring.

performer has to think a little quicker and work a little harder. When one does several headsprings in a row, the knees have to be bent on the landing of each except the last in the series, which can be completed with an arched back. The number of headsprings in the routine can be left up to the individual tumbler, but there is not much point in doing more than four.

SERIES B

1. Roundoff. This stunt was described in Routine II–A.

2. Back Handspring (Fig. 2–16). This is undoubtedly the most important tumbling stunt in advanced competition. It is the stunt that separates advanced and intermediate tumblers. The body should be well off-balance backward for the back handspring. This means that the legs have to be cut under the center of gravity on the snap-down from the roundoff. The back handspring should be taught first from a stationary standing position and not following a roundoff.

TEACHING TECHNIQUES. The tumbler stands erect with arms raised forward to shoulder height and palms down (1). The first movement is to swing the arms downward and backward and to bend the knees. The body should remain almost vertical. In this position the tumbler is off-balance and would fall on the mat if she tried to stop (2). It is a mistake to carry the knees forward so that an on-balance position can be maintained. It is also a bad mistake to lean forward from the waist rather than maintain an almost vertical body position. The first part of the stunt can be practiced by placing a chair in the right position to support the weight in this off-balance position. A partner's knee will serve the same purpose as the chair.

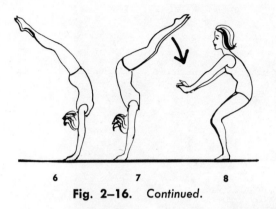

6   7   8

Fig. 2–16. *Continued.*

A partner might also stand directly behind the performer and support the weight by placing a hand on the performers back as this first movement is practiced. Another common mistake is for the performer to sit too low so that the buttocks almost scrape the ground. The thighs should form an angle of about 30 degrees or 35 degrees with a horizontal line drawn through the knees. From this position the arms are swung vigorously upward and backward and as they reach the verticle position the head is also thrown backward very rapidly (3). About the same time the legs straighten quickly and thrust away from the mat and the chest and stomach arch up toward the ceiling (4). The feet leave the ground just slightly before the hands make contact with the mat (5). At the time the hands contact the mat the body is still in an arched position with the hips thrust forward and the legs trailing (6). It is a common mistake to start flexing at the waist, or the knees, too soon in an attempt to get the feet over to the mat. After a fraction of a second delay in this arched position with the hands on the mat the body is quickly flexed at the waist and the feet snapped down to the mat (7, 8). There is also a thrust from the fingers and shoulders to lift the upper body away from the mat.

It is a good technique for students who lack flexibility to practice backbends each practice session before trying back handsprings. It is necessary for other students to practice the leg drive alone. This is done by having them swing their arms above the head and jump upward and backward from the off-balance position without executing the back handspring.

SPOTTING. The best way to spot a beginner for a back handspring is to put her in either an overhead safety belt or a hand belt. A belt suspended from pulleys is an essential piece of equipment

Spotting for a Back Handspring Using an Ordinary Towel. A towel can be substituted for a spotting belt if a belt is not available.

for teaching advanced trampoline work and a very desirable piece of equipment for teaching advanced tumbling especially if heavy girls are to be spotted. A light person can easily spot a heavy individual with an overhead safety belt. The correct way to use a hand belt is to hold the ropes behind the tumbler with one hand very close to her waist. When the back handspring is attempted after a roundoff, the two spotters must run with the tumbler on her approach. The ropes must be wound one-half turn around the performer's waist so that they will unwind as the roundoff is executed. Two towels placed one in front and one behind and then twisted together will serve the purpose of a hand belt. After the back handspring is partially learned, other methods of spotting can be used. One method is to have two girls grasp hands or hold a towel behind the performer so that when she does the back-handspring they can lift under the small of her back. Another method is to have two girls kneel, one on each side of the performer, and lift under the lower back. This method is usually used after the stunt has been practiced in the belt but before the girl is quite ready to do it on her own.

3. Back Extension Roll. This stunt is described in Routine II–A.

4. Fishflop, Squat Through, Snap-Up. These stunts are described in Routine III–B.

SERIES C

Cartwheel, Cartwheel, Roundoff, Back Handspring Walkout with Half Turn, Handspring, Headspring. There are no new stunts in this series, but the combination of stunts is quite difficult, especially the transition from the back handspring to the front-handspring.

The first cartwheel should be done from a run and a skip takeoff (see Routines I–B and II–B). As the second cartwheel is completed, there has to be a quarter turn and pivot on the first foot that touches so that the performer is facing in the right direction for the roundoff. It takes considerable more leg strength to do a good back handspring after a roundoff that follows several other stunts in a series than after one that is the first stunt in a series.

The start of the back handspring is the same as previously explained (see Routine IV–B). The finish, however, is different. Instead of snapping both legs down together, one leg is snapped down ahead of the other. (The right leg is first in this description.) As the right leg is snapped down, a turn to the left is started. When the right foot touches the mat the turn is continued with a pivot on the foot so that a 180° turn is completed. The weight of the body quickly shifts from this right foot to the left foot, which is placed on the mat about two feet in front of the right foot.

In this position the performer is ready for a front handspring (Routine III–A). This handspring is much more difficult than the one previously explained as it has to be done from almost a stationary position. The last stunt in the series, the headspring, should be completed with legs together and back arched.

This routine will take considerable practice before it can be executed as a continuous series with a reasonable amount of speed. Remember, all tumbling series should be continuous and fast. The other routines described up to this point can be executed without much practice once the stunts have been learned. This series, however, even though the stunts have all been completely learned, will still cause trouble for the tumbler. Considerable practice will have to be devoted to the transitions between the stunts.

V. ADVANCED ROUTINE IN DETAIL

SERIES A

Roundoff and a Series of Back Handsprings.   Neither of these stunts is new. Back handsprings in series, however, are much more difficult than a single back handspring. The most important thing when doing this stunt in series is to snap the feet down so that they land in front of the center of gravity when they touch the mat. This means the body will be off-balance backward. This is true for the landing of the feet on the roundoff as well as the back handsprings. At the time the hands contact the mat they also should be cut under the shoulders so that the arms are at least vertical. Actually it might be better if the hands are cut under so that the arms are slightly beyond the vertical position. Fig. 2–17 makes this position clear. Good shoulder flexibility will make this position much easier to

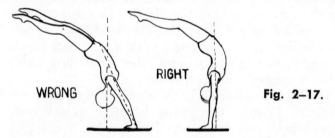

WRONG   RIGHT   Fig. 2–17.

attain.   Students should practice rocking back and forth in the backbend position and do other shoulder flexibility exercises if they lack this quality.

Back handsprings should cover quite a bit of distance. It is hard to say how much distance because of differences in body size and in back and shoulder flexibility. Back handsprings should also be fast and lively. A performer should be able to bounce up in the air as she lands, or work quickly into another back handspring. Sometimes, however, if too much speed is attempted, the back handsprings will become too low, the tumbler will get on balance and the series will bog down. Back handsprings should not be too high but should be high enough so that both hands and feet can be cut under the center of gravity so that each stunt is started with the tumbler off-balance backward.

Another thing very important in a successful series of back handsprings is to let the legs trail or hang behind the chest and stomach. The snap-down to the feet should be accomplished with a hard flexion at the waist with almost a straight leg rather than with the knees leading in a bent leg position. Starting the flexion at the waist too early, especially if the knees are also allowed to bend, is a very bad mistake and makes a good fast series of back handsprings almost impossible.

SERIES B

Handspring with a Walkout, Handspring with a Walkout, Roundoff, Back Handspring Walkout with a Half-Turn, Handspring. None of these stunts is new. The walkout landing (Fig. 2–18) on the front hand-

RIGHT
HIPS FORWARD

WRONG
HIPS BACK

Fig. 2–18. Walkout landing.

spring, however, is fairly difficult and requires some explanation. Before attempting a walkout or stepout landing, the tumbler should be able to execute a high handspring to a landing with the legs straight and the body vertical. Once this has been learned, the walkout is accomplished by spreading the legs slightly before the landing so that one foot touches the mat just before the other. It is important to keep the hips forward and the landing leg almost straight.

If the hips are flexed or the knee bent, it takes a very strong leg to bear the weight. Usually this will result in the leg bending still further as the foot makes contact with the mat. It is not only very poor form, but it becomes almost impossible to execute another handspring if the knees or hips bend too much. A spotter should be used to lift under the performer's back when the walkout handspring is being learned, even though the performer can execute a good handspring with a two-foot landing.

SERIES C

Front Somersault, Head Springs in Series. The front somersault (Fig. 2–19) is a difficult stunt for girls. Some girls will never ac-

1a   1b   1c

Fig. 2–19.   Arm motion for front somersault.

complish a good front somersault and thus might instead have to start this routine with a handspring. The word "flip" is a common gymnastic term for somersault that is now accepted by most authorities.

The front somersault starts with a hard run, a low hurdle, and two-foot takeoff. The hurdle should be an extension of the run rather than a jump before takeoff. The body is almost vertical with the head up at the time of takeoff. The feet should be slightly ahead of the center of gravity. This position of the feet will help change the forward run to upward movement for a good high somersault.

There are three common arm movements used for the front somersault. These would be difficult and lengthy to describe but can be presented in the form of a drawing quite easily (Fig. 2–19 (1a, 1b, 1c)).

In (1a) the arms reach up and then pull forward into the tuck.

2   3   4   5

Fig 2–19.   Continued.   Front somersault.

In (1b), the elbows lead and the motion of the arms is backward and then upward and forward. In (1c), the arms lift up and then pull forward and downward into the tuck. Whatever method is used, the arms must be coordinated with the takeoff to provide height and forward spin.

After the takeoff the head tucks forward onto the chest and the hips lift hard backward and upward (2, 3). The legs are bent and a tuck position is assumed (3, 4). In arm motion "a" and "c" the hands almost always grab the shins in the tuck position, but in arm motion "b" they probably will not make contact with the legs. It is hard to explain exactly when to open out of the tuck for the landing. The tumbler can't see the ground but must time the opening of the tuck (4, 5).

TEACHING TECHNIQUES. Teach the stunt first on the trampoline. If a trampoline is not available, teach it off a spring board or from a reuther board.

SPOTTING. The front somersault will require very careful spotting. A handbelt should be used. If the front somersault has been learned on another piece of equipment, a good hand spot should be sufficient, however. The hand closest to the performer as she approaches is placed under the stomach or hips to give spin and lift. The other hand is placed under the neck or upper back. Extra mats should be used to provide a soft landing area. If plenty of mats are available, they can be stacked quite high, or rolled, to provide an exceptionally high and soft area and then spotting is not quite so essential.

SERIES D

Roundoff, Back Handspring, Back Somersault. The first two stunts in this series are exactly the same as the first two stunts in routine V–A.

The new stunt in this series is the back somersault. Probably the easiest type of back somersault for a girl to learn is a "whip-back" or "throw-back" (Fig. 2–20). This is not a high back somersault and does not require as much leg strength and power to execute as a "tuck-back." It is really just a high back handspring in which the hands are unable to reach the ground. The arm throw is the same as for the back handspring. Most of the turning motion comes from this arm throw which carries well back behind the head (1, 2). When the arch is reached in the air, the hips are quickly flexed so as to bring the feet rapidly over to the mat (3–5). Teaching a whip-back first in the back somersault progression often makes it

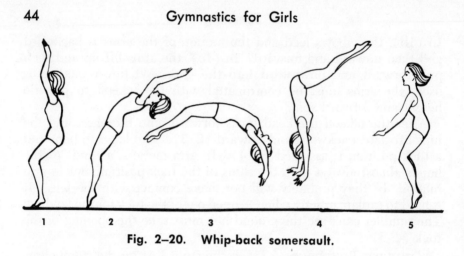

Fig. 2–20.   Whip-back somersault.

difficult for a girl to learn a high tuck or high layout back somersault.   Teachers should be aware of this and use the whip-back with
caution.

TEACHING TECHNIQUES.   This stunt can be taught much easier on
the trampoline and then transferred to the tumbling mat.   Although
it is probably harder to do from a standing position than after a
back handspring, it should be practiced first from a stand.   Another
girl can give an assist by lifting under the feet of the performer.
The girl giving the lift sits in a straddle position on the mat and
places her hands, palm up, on the mat.   The performer stands on this
girl's hands and is assisted by a lift at the time of the spring from the
mat.

SPOTTING—An overhead safety belt or a hand belt should be used
in teaching the back somersault.   When the performer gets good
enough to come out of the belt the stunt should be spotted by hand
for several trials in the same manner as the back handspring.

The Tuck-Back Somersault (Fig. 2–21).   This is a better back
somersault than the whip-back to use as the last stunt of a routine.
The starting position should be almost on balance (1).   In the tuck-
back the arms lift straight up in the air or even stop slightly before
they reach the vertical position.   The arms in this type of somersault help give height but do not contribute to the spin.   The turning
motion comes from a chest lift or backward lean of the upper torso
and head.   The body should remain almost vertical at the time of the
takeoff; that is, the center of gravity should be only slightly behind
the feet.   The backward lean should definitely come only from the
upper torso and not from the waist (2).   As the height of the jump
is reached, the knees pull up rapidly to the chest in a tight tuck and
the hands grasp the shins in this position (3, 4).   The spin is started

with the body stretched and long. When the knees pull up into a tuck, the radius is shortened. The spinning motion therefore speeds up around the axis of rotation. As the somersault is completed, the tuck is released and the body straightened for the landing (5).

1 2 3 4 5

Fig. 2–21.   Tuck-back somersault.

TEACHING TECHNIQUES. The same teaching techniques for a whip-back apply to a tuck-back. However, a circular arm motion is recommended for a tuck back when it is practiced from a stand. The arms are swung down the side and then up the front of the body for the lift. The biceps, or front of the arm, should lead as the arms reach up above the head. The placement of the feet on the back handspring preceding the whip-back is the same as for a back hand-spring that precedes another back handspring. In other words they are cut under so as to have the center of gravity behind the feet. The placement of the feet for a tuck-back somersault is different. The feet should not be cut under but should be snapped down so that the center of gravity is slightly in front of the feet. This posi-tion will result in a higher back somersault.

SPOTTING. The spotting for the tuck-back is the same as for the whip-back.

OTHER ADVANCED STUNTS

There are several other very common stunts or combinations of stunts that should be mentioned for the advanced tumbler. All of these could be added to the four series in group V with very little change in the pattern of the series.

1. Layout Back Somersault. This is an arched back somersault that is somewhat of a combination of the whip-back and the tuck-back. It can also be taught much easier on the trampoline than on the tumbling mats. The leg placement is the same as for the tuck-back because height is needed for this type of somersault. The arm motion is a combination of the other two arm motions described. The arms must lift up as well as pull backward. Usually after the upward lift they go out to the side. A hard chest and stomach lift and a strong backward pull of the head is essential in a layout somersault. A hand belt should be used in teaching this stunt.

2. Whip-Backs in Series. Whip-backs in a row add greatly to the value of a tumbling routine. It is a difficult series for a girl to learn as it requires considerable leg strength. Learning two or more somersaults in a row requires practice and the development of legs strong enough for the task. Use a handbelt in teaching this series.

3. Handspring, Front Somersault. Actually this combination is easier for many girls than a running front somersault alone. If a front handspring can be executed so that considerable rebound can be obtained on the landing, the rebound will take the place of leg strength in obtaining height. The handspring can be finished with either a two-foot landing or a walkout landing. The arm lift for the somersault is similar to the first arm lift described for the front somersault in Routine V–C. A handbelt should be used in teaching this combination.

4. Full-Twisting Back Somersault. Once a good layout somersault has been learned, a twisting somersault may be attempted. This stunt will not be described in this chapter as it is described in the trampoline chapter. It should be taught first on the trampoline. A twisting belt is a very desirable teaching aid in teaching a twisting somersault but is not essential. The ropes of a regular belt can be wound around the performer so that they unwind as the twist is executed.

3

Floor Exercises

It might be a good idea to begin by defining "floor exercises." [1]
To clamp an exact definition upon the term is an impossible task, but
we can say that it is an Olympic event performed in an area of approximately forty feet by forty feet, involving a routine that lasts
from one minute to one and a half minutes. Basically, it contains
elements of dance combinations, poses, acrobatics, and tumbling,
grouped in rhythmical and coherent patterns. Through these and
other movements the gymnast explores the many dimensions of
speed, height, distance, mood, direction, and form. Here lies the
art of gymnastics.

The gymnast faces few restrictions when she walks onto the floor
exercise area. Her skill must work in a limited amount of time and
space. The music must be appropriate to the style and the combinations. A winning routine shows knowledge of the latest trends in
international gymnastics. Form and difficulty must be present. The
only other limitations are internal ones, the ones inherent in the
human body and those which the mind places on the body through
inhibitions and lack of confidence.

This event requires no "secondary" medium such as parallel bars,
balance beam, or horse. The medium is provided by the individual
and is called the "primary" medium. Is it not the most natural
symbol of communication? It encompasses feelings that travel far
beyond the boundaries of human speech.

Floor exercises should not be a showcase for female strength. Its
purposes are to display grace, the grace which only a woman
possesses, to reflect perfection through form which only a well-

---

[1] Other common names for the event are "floor exercise," "free exercise," "free
standing exercises," and "free calisthenics." But, since the official name is "floor exercises," it will be used in the following explanations and descriptions.

disciplined mind possesses, and to express understanding of beauty through striking combinations and effective use of the body's alignment.

The vocabulary of the body is its parts, each of which has power to speak and add accentuation. The limbs, the torso, the head, and facial expressions, in fact every section of the body which is capable of motion or capable of influencing the total effect should receive attention in style development. Even the hair, its movement or lack of it, and its placement has influence.

Unfortunately, American young people have had little exposure to even the most basic gymnastic skills. Instructors must take this into consideration when encountering any lack of interest or anxiety about participation in this physical activity. The teacher must inspire confidence and provide a stimulus for the students to appreciate and to develop these skills. She can point out the immensity of transfer from other sports to gymnastics, floor exercises in particular. Students are less likely to "freeze" at the thought of performing a routine or even an individual stunt, if they are aware of the similarities between this activity and other sports. They can be reminded of the typical movements of basketball—jumping, running, stretching—all are common to almost every physical activity. The teacher might also point out the interelatedness of dance to gymnastics, floor exercises in particular. They are almost inseparable. Both are channels of attaining body understanding. The music that accompanies floor exercise routines is also used in dance.

The teacher might want to mention the values derived from the development of floor exercise skills. One might call a few to mind, such as poise, grace, suppleness, expression, balance, agility, and rhythm. For the talented and hard working often come skills of composure, imaginative composition, and unique stylization.

The observer sees the master gymnast release an outpouring of spiritual energy in her performances. But such efforts are useless encased in form, the child of a well-disciplined mind and an adequate knowledge of skill. One may acquire form by training the body to react effectively to the desires and commands of the mind. The poses scattered throughout a floor exercises routine develop balance and correct body alignment, as well as beauty of presentation.

The teacher may have an opportunity to direct a potential champion of gymnastics. An unusually talented person in the field moves with ease and expression. Her body is strong, flexible, and well proportioned. A good foundation of dance and basic gymnastic skills should be recommended.

Generally speaking, the task of the instructor in floor exercises is to approach the unit effectively. First of all, she should survey the

Photo by Wm. Green; World Telegram and Sun

Betty Jean Maycock in a Typical Floor Exercise Pose. This pose with the weight on the front leg and the other toe pointing backward is used in several routines in the floor exercise chapter. Miss Maycock (Kent, Ohio) is one of the top all-round performers in the U.S. She excels in the floor exercise event and has won the National Championship in the side horse vault. She was a member of the 1960 Olympic team and the U.S. National teams of 1961 and 1962 that toured Europe.

needs and abilities of the group, testing for such basic skills as limberness, coordination, strength, gracefulness, extension, form, balance, and other important prerequisites.

In some areas special tests have not yet been devised, so a subjective evaluation must be made on the basis of observations of students' hopping, stepping, skipping, running, leaping, jumping, turning, and tumbling. As each gymnast performs a set of steps the instructor should analyze the ability in approximate terms.

Needless to say, the body must be prepared to receive the many demands of skill that floor exercises will place upon it. From this point, nourish the body with a strong foundation by a complete developmental fitness program. Let the students know that the body is many separate, individual parts capable of moving in innumerable ways. This should be explained as soon as the various body parts are introduced into the preparatory calisthenics program. In fundamental stages where total body development is stressed, the instructor will want to include stretching, lifting, pushing, and complete relaxation. Body understanding is best reached through use of every set of muscles.

A successful procedure has been to have the class line up and begin by limbering the neck, shoulders, torso, and legs on a walking base. Finish up by jogging for a few minutes, and have the students come to rest in a circle formation. Continue with additional exercises, this time from standing, sitting, and lying positions. It is good to include movements of the head and arms, because control of these more remote body parts is usually slow in development. The more opportunity gymnasts have to use them, the sooner an awareness of their presence and usefulness as a medium of expression will come. As a safety factor, inject adequate use of the knees, ankles, wrists, and neck. They are the object of the most concentrated impact and also are particularly prone to injury.

The more inventive teacher will want to encourage individuality and creative expression as well as excellence of performance. Routines that lack thought often appear mechanical and are by all means a bore to watch. Several methods meet with success. Some encompass very useful group leadership skills.

For example, the instructor presents an exercise to the class and immediately following its execution invites volunteers to demonstrate and lead their variations. Because of a large group or reluctant contributors, another method might be more useful. Ask each to prepare an exercise at home and be ready to demonstrate it in a forthcoming class session. This will give the instructor a glimpse of what exercises appeal to the student. (These might be included when there are lags in class interest.) Of course, the student leadership of exercises can bring about gaps in the material which the teacher plans to cover. In this case, the instructor supplements with additional calisthenics.

Another plan involves assigning sections of the group a certain set of muscles for which they must select and demonstrate appropriate exercises. The most satisfying gymnastic activity is usually done in groups. Ideas can be exchanged more freely as people learn to work with others and accept ideas and criticisms.

Give the group situations in which they may move the body. This involves teaching the basic movements of leaping, jumping, turning, posing, and tumbling. All are situations that require the body to move, the mind to act, and the muscles to respond.

Several elements artistically combined bring to the observer aesthetic pleasure. But only through improvising can the students become in command of a more expressive imagination.

The students should know that form reveals something about the self-discipline of the performer. Form or precision does not come easily. It takes work! But also it takes skillful analysis and correction of mistakes. Have persistence, patience, and the ability to adjust, and eventually form will follow.

What are the major accepted elements of proper gymnastic form? (They should be discussed in class.) Among them are balance, composure, pointed toes, straight knees, full extension, and good body alignment. The one exception to the rule of straight knees is the landing on a dismount or tumbling stunt.

Introduce the competitive exercises as outlined further in the chapter. These routines involve skills on increasing levels of difficulty. You might have the students choose a competitive routine corresponding to their level of achievement, then allow enough time for each gymnast to perfect the stunts.

All those learning the same routine may find the process easier if they work together. Students should discuss each sequence and criticize each other's work. If time allows, practice in judging makes the experience more worthwhile. But be sure to discuss point deductions beforehand.

After each group has learned the routine parallel to its members' ability, let them judge each person's performance. This will make them more aware of their own and other's form breaks. Students being judged can be thinking of attractive presentation along with getting the experience of performing gracefully in front of others.

As an additional assignment, the more ambitious students might want to create their own routine accompanied by music of their own selection. Have them link dance steps and tumbling. For many, such improvising will be a new experience. In the process we shall hope that each discovers for herself the limitless possibilities of movement. Explain continuity—the necessary fitting together of one movement into the next. In other words, high heels are an inappropriate mate to an outfit of blue jeans and sweat shirt. By the same token, each movement must flow easily into the next, the routines being consistent with body type, style, and level of achievement. Well-practiced floor exercises seem natural and are easily controlled, as well as a joy to do.

Both teacher and pupil alike should realize that the routines presented are merely points of departure, ideas to build upon. They make use of some very basic elements of routine composition. The writer has worked to select representative moves for progressive levels of achievement. The number of other possible stunts and combinations exceeds description.

Note that each routine strives for a certain degree of variety. No routine can be interesting if characterized by monotony or "sameness." Well-dispersed acrobatics, fast-moving sequences followed by an abrupt stop or lingering pose—all these bring the much needed "change of pace."

The routines described in this chapter belong to someone else; in other words they were not created by the gymnast herself. They are fine as a starting block. But soon, the enthusiast will have grown beyond the combinations offered in this chapter. She will replace the suggested moves with some of her own. And she will revise as new skills are acquired and as new ideas present themselves.

I. BEGINNING ROUTINE IN DETAIL

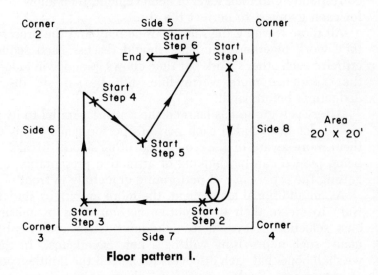

Floor pattern I.

Routine 1 begins in corner number one, close to side number eight. The performer is facing side number seven with the feet together and the arms at the side. Beginning routines normally do not require a full size floor exercise area of 40 feet by 40 feet. This routine is designed to be performed in an area approximately 20 feet by 20 feet.

Step 1 (Fig. 3–1). Step back onto the left foot and circle the

1   2   3

Fig. 3–1. Step 1.

arms overhead (1). Rise onto the toe of the left foot, kicking the right leg forward. Step, and then hop on the right foot, leaning the torso slightly forward and raising the left leg backward to an arabesque position (2). (An arabesque is a one-leg balance with the other leg raised horizontally backward. The body leans forward slightly, but the head and chest should be kept almost vertical.) Take three running steps forward—left, right, left, and leap forward onto the right foot with the arms lifting upward overhead (3). (A good leap should have the dimensions of height and distance. The arms and chest should lift upward to give height to the movement. The landing should be on the ball of the foot with the knee bent to cushion the impact of landing.) Step forward onto the left foot then the right foot. Hop in a circle on the right foot with the left foot held to the side just slightly off the ground and the arms overhead. The performer circles one and one-quarter turns to the right and ends this step facing side number six.

Step 2 (Fig. 3–2). Slide the left foot forward. Close the right foot in back of the left and slide the left foot forward again. Step right, left, and swing the right leg forward and upward, jumping off the left leg to execute a hitch-kick (1, 2). (A hitch-kick is performed by kicking the right leg forward and jumping from the left leg. The legs pass each other in the air much like a scissor high jump in track and field except that the kicking motion is forward instead of to the side. The beauty of the move depends a great deal on the height of the two kicks and on straight legs. The chest and shoulders

Fig. 3–2. Step 2.

should be leaned slightly forward and the arms should lift overhead.)
The landing from the hitch-kick is on the right foot followed quickly
by the left foot, which is placed on the floor in front of the right
foot. Pivot on the left foot one-quarter turn to the right to face
side number five. Raise the arms sideways and the right leg forward (3).

Step 3 (Fig. 3–3). Step right, left, then hop on the left foot,
raising the right knee so that the right foot touches the left knee at
the height of the hop. The arms lift upward during the hop, and the

Fig. 3–3. Step 3.

head bows downward (1). Step forward onto the right foot in a lunge position with the arms circling downward and forward in front of the right foot (2). (In the lunge, most of the body weight is on the right leg, which is directly in front of the body with the knee bent. The left leg is stretched backward with the left foot on the floor.) With the legs still in the lunge position the arms circle overhead and the torso leans back in an arch (3). The body leans forward again, and the hands are placed on the floor (4). The head is tucked and a forward roll is executed to a sitting position on the floor with the legs together and stretched out in front of the body (5). (Refer to Chapter 2 for the forward roll technique.) The arms are raised backward and upward as the body leans forward at the waist with the head almost touching the knees. The legs should remain straight in this position. Raise the upper body to a vertical position, place the hands on the floor to the right of the hips, and turn right to a kneeling position on the floor. This should be a three-eighths turn so that the performer is facing corner number four. Kick the left leg up to the left. The head should turn toward the raised left leg (6). Place the left foot down on the floor in front of the right knee. Stand up, raise the arms overhead, and step on the right foot. Place the weight on the right foot and point the toes of the left foot back. Swing the arms, parallel to each other, downward to the left. Continue the movement of the arms upward to the right, ending with the right arm out to the side and the left arm circled overhead. The torso and the head lean to the right (7).

5   6   7

Fig. 3–3. Continued.

Fig. 3–4. Step 4.

1   2

Step 4 (Fig. 3–4). Step forward on the left foot toward corner number four and execute two "cat jumps." A cat jump is executed by lifting the right leg into the air with the knee bent (1), jumping off the left leg, and raising it with the knee bent (2). The right foot lands first followed quickly by the left.

Step 5. Pivot one-quarter turn to the left on the left foot to face corner number one. Step right and arabesque on the right foot with the arms held straight back. Kick the left leg forward. Pivot one quarter turn to the right on the right foot to end with the left leg lifted to the side. Hop sideways on the right foot, keeping the body

Fig. 3–5. Step 6.

1   2

facing corner number four. Place the left foot on the floor and slide it to the left. Close the right foot to the left foot. Step and hop on the left foot with a half turn left, kicking the right leg sideways toward corner number one. Place the right foot on the floor, close the left foot to a stand on the balls of both feet pivoting one-eighth turn to the left. The feet should be together and the body should be facing side number six.

Step 6 (Fig. 3–5). Step forward onto the right foot raising the arms sideward to shoulder height. Hop on the right foot, kicking the left knee forward with a sharp bend of the left knee (1). Land on the right leg and extend the left leg backward placing the left knee on the floor behind the right foot. Sit down on the left leg and extend the right leg forward. The head bows down to the right leg and the arms stretch backward with the palms facing the floor (2).

II. LOW INTERMEDIATE ROUTINE IN DETAIL

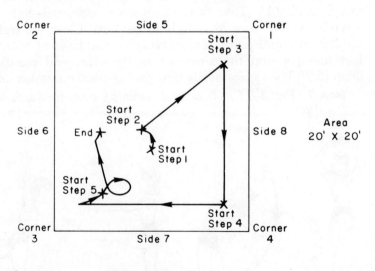

Floor pattern II.

The routine begins in the center of the floor area, the gymnast facing corner number three. As indicated on the floor pattern the area required is only 20 feet by 20 feet rather than the 40 feet by 40 feet prescribed in the rules.

Fig. 3–6. Step 1.

Step 1 (Fig. 3–6).   Start with the feet together, the arms held down at the sides. Rise onto the balls of both feet, leaning the torso to the left. Swing both arms to the left, continuing the motion upward and backward over the head. Finish on the balls of both feet with the arms obliquely upward to the right. The head looks up to the hands (1). Take three small steps backward—left, right, left —making a 180° turn in a circle to the left. Close the right foot to the left foot and pause momentarily on the balls of both feet, the feet together and the arms out to the sides and parallel to the floor (2). The performer is now facing corner number one.

Step 2 (Fig. 3–7).   Take three running steps forward—left, right,

Fig. 3–7. Step 2.

left—and hop on the left foot with the toe of the right foot touching the left knee at the height of the hop and the arms circling overhead (1). Step forward onto the right foot, placing the body weight onto that foot. The toe of the left foot points back. Lower both arms backward past the head and downward while the head and torso lean back in an arch (2). Turn the body one-eighth turn to the left to face side number five. Step back onto the left foot and swing the right foot forward toward side number five (3). Leaving the raised leg in front of the body, circle both arms overhead and pivot 180 degrees left on the left foot to face side number 7. The right leg is now raised in back (4).

Step 3. Step back on the ball of the right foot. Raise the left leg forward, holding the arms out to the sides and parallel to the floor. Step left, right, and arabesque on the right foot. (Refer to Routine I for techniques of performing the arabesque.) The arms are held out to the sides and slightly back. Swing the arms forward, place the hands on the floor in front of the feet, and forward roll to a stand with an immediate jump and half-turn in the air to face

Photo by Wm. Greene; World Telegram and Sun

Betty Maycock in a Split in Floor Exercise. (See photo on page 49 for more information about Miss Maycock.)

Fig. 3–8.   Step 4.

side number five. (The technique for this roll is much the same as for the forward roll described in Chapter 2. The start is slower, however, as the head is lowered slowly to the floor as the left foot is raised high in the air. When the right foot pushes off the floor, the left leg has to be tucked quickly. Spot in the same manner as for a regular forward roll.) Step backward onto the left foot. Swing the right leg backward into an arabesque position, simultaneously hopping backward on the left foot. The left arm is held forward, the right backward in the arabesque. Step backward onto the right foot. Swing the left leg backward into an arabesque position, simultaneously hopping backward on the right foot. The left arm is forward and the right backward in the arabesque.

Step 4 (Fig. 3–8). Pivot one-quarter turn on the right foot to face side number six. Run—left, right, left—and leap onto the right foot (1). Place the left foot beside the right with the arms held at the sides. Execute a body wave by bending the knees and hips slightly and letting the entire body sag. The head, shoulders, and upper torso should droop forward (2). Raise the arms forward and upward and at the same time rise on the toes stretching high in an arch (3). Swing the arms downward and backward, while the body is in the arch (4). Continue bringing the arms downward toward the floor and bend the knees so that both hands can be placed on the floor in front of the feet (5). Tuck the head and roll backward to the feet. (Refer to Chapter 2 for techniques of the backward roll.) Just as the feet are about to touch the floor, spread the legs to land in a straddle position (6). Lift the hands from the floor and straighten the torso to a vertical position. Turn the right

Fig. 3–8. *Continued.*

foot and the torso one-quarter turn to face side number five, bend the left knee, drop the head backward, and arch the back. Hold this backward lunge position momentarily with the right arm out to the side and the left arm circled overhead (7). Straighten the body, closing the left foot to the right foot.

Step 5 (Fig. 3–9). This step starts facing side number five. Walk several steps in a circle making a full turn to the right to face side number five again. While the walking steps are performed, the right arm is circled overhead, and the left arm is held out to the side, and the head and torso are leaned toward the right arm. Step toward side number five—left, right—and hitch kick. (Refer to Routine I for an explanation of the hitch kick.) Step onto the left foot and pivot one-eighth turn right. Bend the left knee and bow the head toward the right knee with the arms held straight back. The eyes look back to the right hand in this finishing pose (1).

Fig. 3–9. Step 5.

III. INTERMEDIATE ROUTINE IN DETAIL

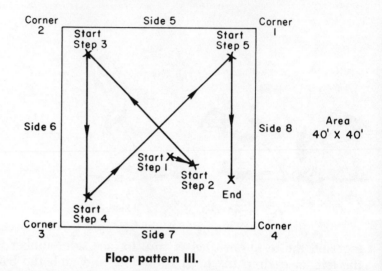

Floor pattern III.

The routine begins about ten feet from corner number four. The performer stands facing into the corner with both feet together and the hands down at the sides. A full size floor exercise area, 40 feet by 40 feet, is used for this routine and for the next two routines in the chapter.

Step 1. Step forward onto the right foot, with the arms circling overhead. Execute a half turn left, pivoting on the right foot to face corner number two. The arms lower downward to a position parallel to the floor.

Fig. 3–10. Step 2.

Step 2 (Fig. 3–10). Step onto the left foot and raise the right leg backward into a scale with the arms held obliquely downward and backward (1). (A scale is very similar to an arabesque. It is a one leg balance with the other leg raised horizontally backward. The upper body and head are also lowered to a position almost horizontal to the floor.) Gradually rise onto the ball of the left foot. This is a pose and should be held momentarily. Step forward onto the right foot. Step left and hitch kick. (Refer to routine number one for a detailed explanation of the hitch kick.) Kick the right leg forward toward corner number two, lift the arms overhead (2), and cartwheel to the right. (The cartwheel is executed by dropping the right foot to the floor and placing first the right hand then the left hand on the floor. The left foot lands first then the right foot.) (Refer to Chapter II for a detailed explanation of the cartwheel.) The cartwheel ends in a lunge position with the right leg bent and the left leg stretched backward. The torso is turned to face the right leg which points toward corner number two. Circle the arms in front of the chest, and then open them out to a sideward position. The upper body and head should lean backward in the lunge (3). Keep both arms extended out to the sides, tuck the head, and roll forward toward corner number two without placing the hands on the floor (4). Roll up to the feet and immediately jump in the air making a three-eighths turn to the left to face side number seven. (The forward roll looks best when the arms are directly out to the side and horizontal to the floor. It is important to stay in a tight tuck and to keep the momentum going forward by leaning the head and shoulders forward as the roll is completed.)

3 4

Fig. 3–10. *Continued.*

1   2   3

Fig. 3–11. Step 4.

Step 3. Step forward onto the right foot and close the left foot behind the right foot. Slide the right foot forward and hop on the right foot as the left leg lifts backward and upward. Raise the arms obliquely upward with the right arm slightly higher than the left. Step forward onto the left foot and close the right foot behind the left foot. Slide the left foot forward and hop on the left foot as the right leg lifts backward and upward. Raise the arms obliquely upward with the left arm slightly higher than the right. Take two running steps—right, left—and leap onto the right foot. Immediately cross the left foot over the right foot, making a five-eighths turn to the right on the balls of both feet. End facing corner number one.

Step 4 (Fig. 3–11). Raise the left leg forward. Step onto the left foot and hop, lifting the arms straight overhead and the toe of the right foot to the left knee at the height of the hop (1). Step-hop on the right foot, both arms lifting upward once more. Step forward on the left foot and pivot one-half turn right on the ball of the foot. End with the body weight on the left leg with the knee bent and point the right foot forward toward corner number three. Bend forward at the waist so the forehead is near the right knee (2). Tuck the head and backward roll to a straddle position with the trunk bent forward parallel to the floor and the arms out to the sides (3). Lift both hands overhead and raising the body to a vertical position. Turn the torso to face the right leg. Slide the legs down into a split, the right leg stretched forward, the left leg stretched backward, and the torso facing corner number two (4).

4   5
Fig. 3–11. *Continued.*

Circle both arms in front toward the right knee. Continue the
arm movement out to the sides and back. Close the legs together
so both legs are stretched directly in front of the body pointing
toward corner number three. Backward roll to a stand. (Refer to
Chapter 2 for an explanation of the backward roll.) Jump backward to an arabesque on the right leg with the leg bent and the
left leg stretched backward (5). Hop backward on the right foot,
keeping the body in the arabesque position. On the hop the left
arm is held forward and the right arm is stretched backward. Hop
again with a one-eighth turn to face side number seven and land on
both feet with the arms out to the sides.

Step 5 (Fig. 3–12). Take several running steps toward side num-

Fig. 3–12. **Step 5.**

1

ber seven, skip, and execute a roundoff. (This stunt should be done to appear light and quick with lots of life. See Chapter 2 for a detailed description of the roundoff.) Land on two feet on the roundoff but immediately step backward onto the left foot. The torso leans backward over the left foot and the right foot points forward. The right arm is held out to the side and the left arm is circled overhead (1). End the routine by closing the right foot to the left foot and lowering the arms to the sides.

IV. LOW ADVANCED ROUTINE IN DETAIL

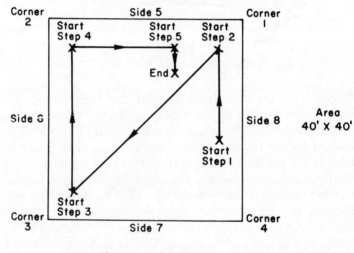

Floor pattern IV.

The routine begins close to side number eight, approximately midway between corner number one and corner number four. Stand on the right foot with the left foot pointed backward. The left arm is held out to the side and the right arm is circled overhead.

Step 1. Step backward onto the left foot lowering the right arm down in front and the left arm down in back. Brush the right foot forward off the ground and jump onto the right foot with the knee bent and the left leg stretched backward. The left arm is held forward and the right arm backward. Step backward on the left leg again, brush the right foot forward off the ground, and jump onto the right foot again with the knee bent and the left leg stretched backward. Step forward onto the left foot. Brush the right foot

Fig. 3–13. Step 2.

forward and slightly off the ground. Jump off the left foot and execute a three-eighths turn left in the air, landing on both feet facing corner number three.

Step 2 (Fig. 3–13). Immediately jump to a pose on the balls of both feet with the right foot placed in front of the left foot. The feet should be very close together with the left arm raised to the side and the right arm circled overhead (1). Sway the trunk to the right and swing the left arm overhead as the right arm drops to a horizontal position (2). Reverse the swaying motion of the trunk to the left with the right arm circled overhead and the left arm out to the side. Return both arms to a circle position overhead (3). Take four running steps—right, left, right, left—lowering the arms downward. Leap onto the right leg with the left arm forward and the right arm back. Step and hop on the left foot, swinging the arms overhead and touching the right foot to the left knee at the height of the hop. Step forward onto the right foot and execute a front handspring. (Refer to Chapter 2 for an explanation of the front handspring.) Land on both feet, then cross the left foot over the right foot and pivot three-eighths of a turn right on the left foot to face side number five.

Step 3 (Fig. 3–14). Step forward onto the right foot. Lower the torso forward and raise the left leg backward into a scale. (Refer to the intermediate routine for a description of the scale.) Lower the left leg and raise the torso with both arms straight overhead. Step back onto the left foot and lower both arms. Step backward onto the right foot so that the ball of the foot touches the floor about six inches in back of the left heel. Place the body weight onto the right foot and lift the left leg, with the knee straight and the

Fig. 3–14.   Step 3.

toes pointed, slightly off the floor in front of the right foot. Step onto the left foot. Step forward onto the ball of the right foot, lifting the left leg backward into a slight arabesque. The right arm is held obliquely upward and forward and the left arm obliquely downward and backward (1). (In the next few steps the performer makes a complete turn to the right along the line of direction by pivoting first on the left foot then the right foot.) Step forward onto the left leg crossing it over the right leg. Step forward onto the ball of the right foot crossing it in back of the left foot with the knee bent. Straighten the right knee lifting the left foot slightly off the floor and step onto the left foot, crossing it in front of the right. Kick the right leg toward side number five, drop it to the floor, and execute a one-arm cartwheel to the right (2). (Refer to Chapter 2 for a description of the two-arm cartwheel. Since only one arm is used to support the body weight in this cartwheel, it is especially important that the elbow of the supporting arm be perfectly straight or "locked.") Begin another cartwheel using both hands (3) but stop when the body reaches a handstand and hold this position momentarily (4).

Step 4 (Fig. 3–15). Tuck the head, bend the arms, and lower the back of the neck to the floor, roll forward straddling the legs wide apart during the roll, and end in a straddle stand. The roll will be in the direction of side number eight. Raise and then turn the torso toward the right leg and lower down into a split with the right leg forward. Turn the torso one-quarter turn to the left and return to the previous straddle position facing side number eight. Forward roll to a stand with the feet close together. Jump off the floor with both feet, lean the body forward, land on the right foot, and

Fig. 3–15. Step 4.

1

swing the left leg backward to a scale. Swing the left leg downward and forward from the scale and walk toward side number eight—left, right, left—and then kick the right leg forward into the air, immediately followed by the left leg. Land on the left foot and step forward onto the ball of the right foot. (This step is very similar to the hitch-kick except the legs do not scissor in the air. The spring is off the left foot and the landing is also on the left foot. The left foot rises up to the right foot in the air and then immediately returns to the floor while the right leg remains in the air.) Raise the left leg backward slightly off the floor, hold the right arm obliquely forward, and upward and the left arm out to the side at shoulder height. Execute a three-quarter turn to the right on the ball of the right foot to face side number five while holding this pose (1). (Correct posture is vital in making this turn. The hips should be forward and the stomach flat with the body in a straight line.)

Step 5 (Fig. 3–16). Step forward toward side number five onto the left foot. Swing the right leg forward, pivoting one-half turn

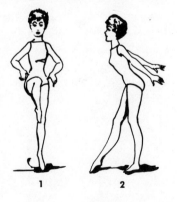

Fig. 3–16. Step 5.

1   2

to the right on the left foot with the toe of the right foot touching the left knee (1). Straighten the right leg, extend it forward, and place the toe on the floor in front of the left foot. Bend forward slightly at the waist, bow the head and hold the arms obliquely backward and downward (2). This routine ends facing side number seven.

V. ADVANCED ROUTINE IN DETAIL

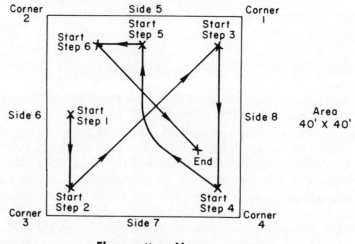

Floor pattern V.

This routine starts close to side number six midway between corners two and three facing side number five.

Fig. 3–17. Step 2.

Step 1. Traveling backward toward side number seven, step and hop on the right foot with the left leg held backward in an arabesque position. The right arm is held out to the side and the left arm is stretched forward. Still traveling backward, step and hop on the left foot with the right leg held backward in an arabesque position. The left arm is held out to the side and the right arm is stretched forward. Turn 180 degrees to the right on the ball of the left foot. Take two long running steps—right, left—swinging the arms down at the sides and leap onto the right leg and hold a momentary scale.

Step 2 (Fig. 3–17). Step forward onto the left foot. Cross the right foot over the left foot making a five-eighths pivot turn left on the left foot to face corner number one. Step right, left—then kick the right leg forward (1) and jump into the air, making a half turn left in the air with the arms circling overhead. Land on the right leg facing corner number three (2). Immediately pivot one-half turn to the left on the ball of the right foot to face corner number one again. This step is called a tour jeté. (The tour jeté should not appear stiff or jerky but rather should have a flowing and floating quality. The arms should be used to get height and the landing should be light.) Take a few running steps and execute an aerial walkover (3–6). (An aerial walkover is a special type of front somersault done in an arched position with a takeoff from one leg and a landing on one leg. In this description the stunt is explained with a takeoff from the right foot. The performer hops on the left foot with the right foot raised in front as for a handspring. The right foot is placed forcefully on the ground and the left leg is thrown vigorously backward and upward. The right leg thrusts off the ground and the arms lift backward and upward. The legs circle one at a time over the head with the back in an exaggerated arch.

3   4   5   6

Fig. 3–17. *Continued.*

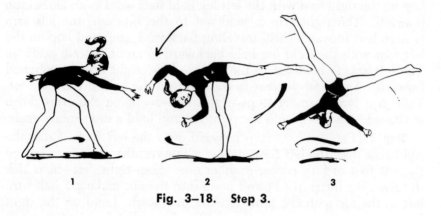

Fig. 3–18. Step 3.

The landing is on the left foot followed by the right foot. This stunt should be spotted with an overhead safety belt or with a hand belt during the learning process.) After the landing on the left and then the right leg, step forward onto the left foot, bending the left knee. (Note: If the aerial is done off the left leg, an extra step will have to be taken after the landing in order to continue with the routine as described.) Slide and close the right foot in back of the left foot with the right heel slightly lifted from the floor and the right knee bent. Step backward onto the right foot and pivot three-eighths of a turn to the right on the balls of both feet.

Step 3 (Fig. 3–18). Cartwheel to the right on one hand, landing first on the left foot then the right. (Refer to the low advanced routine in this chapter for an explanation of the one arm cartwheel.) Turn to the right, pivoting 180 degrees on the balls of the right foot as it lands from the cartwheel, and then 180 degrees on the left foot. Execute another pivot turn in the same manner traveling along side number eight. Step onto the right foot again, continuing to pivot right, and execute a "butterfly" to the right (1–5).

(The preparatory movement is very important for this stunt. Practice it before trying the whole stunt. Stand with the feet apart and the body bent almost 90 degrees forward at the waist. Sway the entire body from right to left in an effort to gather momentum for the butterfly to the right. The stunt is executed by jumping off the right foot dropping the upper body slightly below the horizontal position and landing on the left foot. In the air both legs are raised to a horizontal position. The arms as well as the spring from the right foot should be used to get height. As the left foot lands, the trunk is raised to a vertical position and the pivot to

4 5 6

Fig. 3–18. *Continued.*

the right continues. By the time the right foot contacts the floor another 180 degree turn has been made.) Step forward with the left foot toward side seven and point the toe of the right foot backward. Pause in a pose with the back arched, the right arm straight forward in front of the chest, and the left arm straight upward slightly behind the head (6).

Step 4 (Fig. 3–19). Pivot to the right on the left foot to face corner number two. Stretch the arms to the side about shoulder height. Step right, left, and hop on the left foot, lifting the arms overhead and raising the right leg so that the toe of the right foot touches the left knee. Step and hop on the right foot with the arms circling backward, downward, and upward again. Step left, right, and close the left foot to the back of the right foot with the arms

1 2 3

Fig. 3–19. **Step 4.**

Fig. 3–19. *Continued.*

held straight out to the sides. Pivot three-eighths of a turn to the left to face side seven and execute a back walkover (1–5) to a split with the right leg forward (6, 7). (Before a back walkover is attempted to the split, it should be learned to a foot landing. The walkover starts with the right foot slightly ahead of the left foot. Arch backward reaching over the head for the floor. Stay in balance during the first part of the stunt but as the hands get close to the floor fall the remaining distance onto the hands. During this backward arch the right leg is raised from the floor and extended straight forward. As the hands contact the floor, the left leg pushes strongly off the floor. At this point the weight is supported entirely by the arms in a handstand position with the legs split wide apart. Lower the right leg to the floor from this position. To finish in a split the right leg is lowered directly between the arms and doesn't make contact with the floor until the foot is well in front of the hands.) Turn to the left by pivoting on the right buttock and swing the right leg through an arc of 180 degrees and end in a sitting position with both legs in front of the body facing side five. Roll backward onto the neck, placing the hands on the floor beside the head (8), and neckspring to the feet, landing first on the left foot, then on the right with the right foot landing in front of the left (9). (Refer to Chapter 2 for an explanation of the neck-spring or snap-up.) Slide the left foot forward to the right foot. Slide and hop on the right foot with the left leg held in an arabesque. Step forward and hop on the left foot, bending the left knee with the right leg held in an arabesque. Place the left foot beside the right.

Step 5 (Fig. 3–20). This step starts facing side number five. Jump sideways off both feet toward side six, landing on the left foot with the left knee bent and the right leg stretched out to the

Fig. 3–19. *Continued.*

side slightly off the floor (1). Cross the right foot behind the left foot (2). Step onto the right foot making a pivot turn to the right to face corner number four.

Step 6 (Fig. 3–21). Swing the right leg forward, rising onto the ball of the left foot. Take a few running steps and execute a roundoff, back handspring, back layout somersault. (Refer to Chapter 2 for an analysis of the moves contained in this tumbling sequence.) Step sideways onto the right foot. Place the left foot behind the right foot, stepping onto the ball of the left foot and lifting the right foot slightly off the ground in front. The arms swing in the direction of the movement. Step to the left on the right foot crossing it slightly over the left foot, turn the body and feet a little to the left, and bend the knees slightly. Jump into the air, making a full turn to the right with the arms held close to the front of the

Fig. 3–20. Step 5.

Gymnastics for Girls

Fig. 3–21.   Step 6.

1   2

body and the feet together (1). This is known as a pirouette. (During the full pirouette keep the head up with the eyes looking directly in front.)   Step back onto the right foot, point the toe of the left foot forward, raise the right arm obliquely upward and forward, and place the left arm obliquely downward and backward. The eyes should look toward the raised right hand (2).

4

The Balance Beam

The art of balancing is included in all physical activities performed by man. Balancing apparatus such as balance beams have been used for several hundred years in gymnastics. Early in the seventeenth century, physical educators stressed balancing upon a beam, the edge of a board, or a similar apparatus.

Balance beam exercises on a narrow surface not only require skill in controlling the body, but in girls' competition lead to the development of graceful, feminine movement. For this reason, the balance beam is a very fitting piece of equipment for girls. Although advanced performers need strength and coordination to perform stunts, the stunts they attempt should be performed easily and gracefully— not with the brute force exhibited in men's work.

Of the four events in girls' competition involving apparatus, the author believes that the balance beam is the easiest with which to begin teaching, because beginning routines require only the skill of good balance in moving on a narrow surface. All the girls in a physical education class can be successful in learning a beginning routine on the balance beam—if not on the high beam at least on the low one. Students should not get the idea that the balance beam is an easy event, however, as the advanced stunts require a great deal of practice.

The Amateur Athletic Union Gymnastic Rule Book lists the following specifications for the measurements of a balance beam.

77

Specification	Metric Measure	Linear Measure
Length of beam	5 meters	16 feet 4 inches
Width on top surface	10 centimeters	$3^{15}\!/_{16}$ inches
Height from floor	120 centimeters	3 feet 11 inches
Thickness of beam	16 centimeters	6½ inches

These dimensions also hold true for Olympic competition.

As was mentioned in a previous chapter, it is not necessary to begin with a beam four feet high. In fact, it is preferable to start on a lower beam, before increasing the height, in order that the girls may learn to move freely on a narrow surface. The only disadvantage is that mounts will be virtually impossible, and any stunts that require the legs to swing below the edge of the beam cannot be practiced.

Commercially made beams, as a rule, are adjustable down to a height of approximately two feet. A good height for the beam for teaching purposes is sixteen or eighteen inches from the floor to the top edge. At this height, the performers can step on the beam easily and begin the early skills of walking, running, jumping, skipping, and holding stationary balances. If a fall occurs, recovery is easily accomplished. Nevertheless, the floor should be well padded to minimize injuries. For further safety, check the beam periodically and sand down jagged or split edges. Beware of surface finishes such as varnish or shellac, which could cause performers to slip.

The cost of a commercially made beam may vary in price from two to three hundred dollars. However, this needn't frighten prospective teachers and students, because with a little ingenuity, wood, and glue, a beam can be made for as little as twenty dollars.

The author has the following suggestions for the construction of a homemade beam: (1) Ask the maintenance department in your school district or an industrial arts class to construct a beam for you. (2) Give them the dimensions and a picture of the beam. (3) Select materials that will not deteriorate under hard usage. Cheap wood will warp with time and result in a crooked beam. (4) If necessary, one could apply the finish herself if the construction were completed. If these plans aren't feasible, you can construct a beam yourself, in a week's time, with the help of several students. A large empty room, the necessary materials, some patience, and students willing to do the work is all that is required. Encourage your students to make a beam of their own upon which they can practice—this is something they could work on during the summer months. The results will be surprising.

HOW TO MAKE A BALANCE BEAM

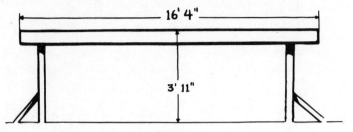

Regulation beam.

Materials Required

Lumber, pieces

3	2″ × 6″ × 16′	Good quality fir, pine, spruce, mahogany—fine grain and free of knots for the main body of the beam.
1	1″ × 5″ × 16′	Birch or maple for a good finished top edge.
1	1″ × 5″ × 16′	Fir, pine, spruce, mahogany for finish on bottom side. Doesn't have to be as good as the top side.
2	2″ × 6″ × 8″	Birch or maple for finished ends.

Glue for Wood

Weldwood or Frankline–Hyde Wood Glue

Supports

Pipe, wood, or wood blocks for standards

Finish

Sanding sealer or a nonslip finish if the beam is used inside and particularly if it is high and used in competition; for a permanent finish if the beam is used out-of-doors, a plastic is suggested.

Special Note

This beam differs from the regulation beam in two ways: 1) it is lower 2) the depth has been increased from 6½ inches to 8 inches because of the materials used. Since this is not a competitive beam, these changes are acceptable and more beneficial for beginning students.

Directions

a) Glue the three pieces of 2″ × 6″ × 16′ together placing the 6″ × 16′ surface one on top of the other. Place the length in vices to assure that the boards will be straight and put weight on the surface top to aid in sealing the glue.

2 × 6
2 × 6
2 × 6

a

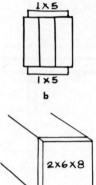

b

b) Turn the beam onto its side and glue the $1'' \times 5'' \times 16'$ birch or maple on the top edge and $1'' \times 5'' \times 16'$ fir, pine, etc., on the bottom edge.

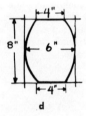

c

c) Glue the $2'' \times 6'' \times 8''$ on both ends to extend the beam to $16' 4''$ and also cover the seams of the $2'' \times 6'' \times 16'$s.

d) Plane down the top edge and bottom edge of the beam to four inches leaving the six-inch thickness through the center.

e) Sand the top and side surfaces and apply the finish. Sanding sealer or any other finish that will not be slippery is suggested.

f) Make a standard to support the beam. (1) Saw horse supports with a bolt down through the beam into the supports; (2) place wooden blocks on top of each other with a threaded rod through the center. The blocks could be added or taken away to adjust the height of the beam; (3) a metal tripod could be used. Check the beam for stability so that it won't sway from side to side or forward and backward. Make the supports level—rubber tips on the bottom are suggested.

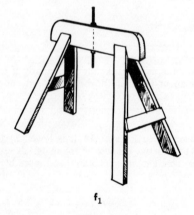

f₁

f₂

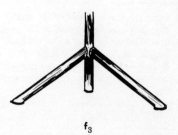

f₃

COMPOSITION OF ROUTINES

In general, routines can be broken down into four parts. The first is entitled the "mount" or the method in which the performer commences the routine or gets up on the beam. When the beam is set at four feet, a run and jump is required in order to get the feet, hips, head, or perhaps another part of the body up on the equipment. To aid in the spring, a beat board or a reuther board may be used. To gain good height in mounts, the performer usually takes off on the board with both feet. Mounts that use a scissoring-type action with the legs require a one-foot takeoff. As a rule, the higher the hips can be lifted on the jump, the easier the mounts involving the placement of the feet or the head on the beam will be. The approaching run need not be lengthy; fifteen to twenty feet should be sufficient.

The last part of the routine, the stunt the performers use to get off the beam, is called the "dismount." Above all, the performer must show that she has good control and balance upon landing. A knee bend to take up the shock is essential. The performer must straighten up after the knee bend and demonstrate good posture. Moving the feet or touching the ground with the hands is considered poor form for which points would be deducted in a competitive meet. The dismounts listed in the following routines permit one hand to remain on the beam during the execution of the stunt, thereby allowing the performer a stabilizing factor upon the landing. The performer should take advantage of this and realize the help it can give her. There is no set pattern as to the place where the dismount should be made, as it can be made from the ends, the center, or any other part of the beam. It would not be wise, however, to land near the supports of the balance beam because of the danger of an injury from the protrusions.

A third category of balance beam work is entitled "stunts on the beam." Among these would be forward rolls, backward shoulder and head rolls, cartwheels, handstands, headstands, walkovers, and splits. These are considered the difficult stunts to learn. Upon mastery, they would be included in a routine. Unless several of these stunts are used in a performer's routine, she would not be awarded a high score in competition.

The fourth category the author entitles "movement." This means the general impression of fluidity, grace, and the manner in which the performer moves between stunts. The "stunts" are not performed directly one after the other but are spaced throughout a routine. Thus, some type of movement is necessary to allow the

Betty Jean Maycock Executing a Forward Kick on the Balance Beam.
(See photo on page 49 for more information about Miss Maycock.)

performer to move to other parts of the beam. Various runs, leaps, turns, and jumps may be employed. Ballet moves are used effectively—walks, turns, and pirouettes artistically executed are a vital part of a balance beam routine. A few "held" or stationary positions may be included, but they must not dominate the routine.

A competitive routine has the minimum time requirement of one and one-half minutes and a maximum of two minutes. However, in a physical education class this time requirement would not be practical for several reasons. Number one, the beginner would not have enough stunts for that length of a routine without repeating. Number two, only a few girls in the class would get a turn because as a rule only one performer can be on the apparatus at a time. A routine could be learned en masse by having the girls practice on a line or board on the floor. This would at least get the routine memorized so that when the performer had her turn on the beam she would not waste time asking questions about what to do next.

SPECIAL NOTE

The requirements for acceptable competitive routines are included in this chapter.

The first three routines are rather definite as to which foot or direction to use. In the fourth and fifth routines, the author feels that more leeway is necessary, since in the more advanced stunts the performer might have a "preferable side" or a "better leg." Thus the student would be free to use her "better" side. In required

Photo by Jim Fraser

Joyce Tanac, Twelve-Year-Old Seattle Sensation, Performing a Lever on the Balance Beam. She was Pacific Northwest Novice Champion in 1962.

routines, the competitor would have to follow the routine specifically as stated or, if she did change it, it would mean a change in the routine in its entirety.

There may be a question as to arm position. Again, in required routines, they would be definitely stated. However, in endeavoring to make the routines as simplified as possible, the author has merely made suggestions in several places. Beginners as a rule are concerned mainly with the proper placement of the feet without the added complication of the arm movement. Ordinarily, the arms to the sides at shoulder level lend the greatest aid toward good balance. In addition, keeping the elbows slightly rounded retains an arm line that is soft. Ballet positions would be very proper. Experimenting with various arm positions is desirable. As a rule, the palms are down, but not always. Keep in mind that the performer wants to create a picture of gracefulness and feminity in the movement of the entire body.

A word can be said here concerning facial expression. Perhaps this is only for those in competition, but it might be a help to beginning students. A pleasant expression, not overbearing, helps to enhance a routine for all those who witness its execution in addition to providing additional confidence to the performer.

SPOTTING

A question asked by all teachers is, "How can I help the performer learn the stunt in the quickest and safest manner?" On the lowered beam the problem is not as great. If the girl jumps clear of the beam, she should have no problem of recovery provided the floor and supports are well padded with mats. However, if only the high beam is available, the performer can be assisted in the following manner. For walking and movement skills, the teacher or spotter may add stability by holding onto her hand; if greater security is needed, have a spotter on each side in order to support each hand. As a rule, the spotter would be standing on the ground, but sometimes she should stand on a chair or even a table to gain the necessary height.

Since the center of gravity for girls is located in the hip region, this is the point to support the performer in nearly all stunts. Place the hands on either side of the hips and lift, push, or help balance as the stunt requires. Usually one spotter is sufficient, but for greater protection place another spotter on the other side to catch the performer should she fall to that side. The spotter must bear in mind her own safety as well. Keep the head well back so it won't be hit by legs or arms that might be moving quickly as some stunts are executed. Most balance beam stunts, as they are learned, should be done very slowly and in a controlled manner so that there is a generous amount of time for thinking and being aware

Photo by Jim Fraser

Gail Sontgerath, Eighteen-Year-Old High School Girl from West Palm Beach, Fla., Performing on the Balance Beam During the 1962 National A.A.U. Championships in Seattle. Miss Sontgerath won the National Senior All-Round Championship in 1960 while only sixteen years of age. She was a member of the 1960 Olympic team, the 1961 National team that toured Europe, and the 1962 U.S. National team that participated in the World Games in Czechoslovakia.

of what the body is doing. This is particularly true when the stunt is being spotted. Above all, give the performer the confidence of doing the stunt carefully and securely so that fear won't cause her to avoid trying it again should a fall occur.

In the pages that follow, the abbreviated descriptions of the routines aid the performer in remembering the sequence. This section is followed by detailed descriptions and illustrations. The beginner should start with the detailed descriptions.

ABBREVIATED ROUTINE DESCRIPTIONS

I. Mount with a front support, right leg around to a straddle sit, toes up behind to stand, three running steps, rise on toes, and half turn, front scale, three dip steps forward, two jump changes, rise on toes, and half turn, three dip steps walking backward, three duck walk steps forward, to knee scale, fence dismount.

II. Mount with single knee balance, quarter turn left to swan balance, stand, two back dip steps, toe stand half turn, two gallop steps forward, leg swing turn, pose, quarter turn to right, three sliding steps placing foot in front, quarter turn, raise single leg high backward to front scale, down to squat position and half turn, knee scale, stand half turn, three forward dip steps, straddle toe touch dismount off the end.

III. Mount with half squat half straddle, quarter turn, stand, three running steps, forward leg swing turn, two running steps to stag leap and front scale, two cat walk steps, corkscrew turn, two steps, squat, forward roll, v-sit, straddle down to toes, stand, step scissors jump, two jump changes, toe stand half turn, body wave, two step-tap-hops, half turn, free sit, backward shoulder roll, knee scale, lift to toe balance, quarter turn, half turn with extended leg, turn half again, stand, leg raise, cartwheel off end.

IV. Straddle mount, quarter turn, splits, straddle sit, lie on beam for backward shoulder roll, single knee scale, stand, rise on toes, leg back for momentary pose, three goose steps forward, step forward, step behind, step forward and pivot on this foot turning half and facing the other direction and hop high on this same foot, two gallop steps forward, two jumps with bent knees, step, half turn, two step-tap-hops, bend to squat, forward roll, swing straddle legs half twist in air to straddle seat facing opposite direction, stand, deep split scale, two sissones, two steps, English handstand near the end of the beam, quarter turn dismount off the end.

V. Mount with a forward roll on the end of the beam, v-sit, one foot forward to stand, three leaps, two squat jumps, stand, swing leg forward, back halfturn corkscrew, pose with one leg forward, two sissones, cartwheel, full pirouette, free sit, backward head roll, pose, half turn split scale, scissors handstand, down to split, lie back to a candle hold, roll forward to stand half turn, one leg raise to cartwheel handstand half turn off center of beam landing on the far side of the beam.

I. BEGINNING ROUTINE IN DETAIL

1. Front Support Mount (Fig. 4–1). Facing the side of the beam, take about five running steps, and take a two-foot takeoff to a front support about the center of the apparatus. Place the weight on both hands, elbows straight, and hips resting against the beam. The fingers are pointing forward gripping the side of the beam, while the thumbs remain on the top.

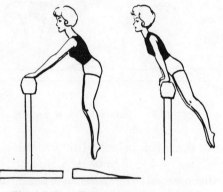

Fig. 4–1. Front support mount.

2. Straddle Sit (Fig. 4–2). Swing the right leg over the beam while turning the body one quarter to the left. Come to a momentary sit straddling the beam.

Fig. 4–2. Straddle sit.

3. Stand from a Squat (Fig. 4–3). Move the legs back and up slowly with the knees bent until the toes of both feet are on the beam. From here simply lift the body up with the hand and toe support to a stand.

SPOTTING. Support the performers arms at the elbows to assure their being straight. Take the hand as the performer stands up.

Fig. 4–3. Stand from a squat.

4. Starting with the left foot, take three running steps—left, right, left. **Pivot Turn** (Fig. 4–4). Then step again on the right foot while rising on the toes, lift the arms overhead, and turn one half so that the performer faces the opposite direction.

Fig. 4–4. Pivot turn.

5. Front Scale (Fig. 4–5). Continue immediately into a front scale. A front scale is a balance on one leg with the other leg raised backward as high as possible without allowing the upper trunk to fall below the level of the hips. The support is on the left leg with the right leg raised. Both legs should be kept straight. Hold this position for at least three seconds.

SPOTTING. Hold the hand.

Fig. 4–5.   Front scale.

6. Dip Steps (Fig. 4–6). Take three dip steps forward—right, left, right. A dip step is a walking step but, as the free leg moves forward, it moves down and brushes the side of the beam and the toe is pointed. The supporting leg at the same time bends slightly which allows the free leg to extend below the top edge of the beam.

SPOTTING. Hold the hand.

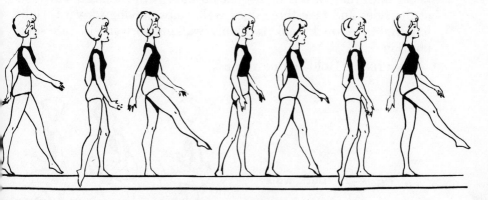

Fig. 4–6.   Dip steps.

7. Jump Change (Fig. 4–7).   Following the dip steps is a "jump change" that involves a jump off both feet allowing the back foot to come forward upon the landing.   Since the right leg is forward, after the jump the left foot is leading.   With a second jump change the right foot is again forward.

Fig. 4–7.   Jump change.

8. Step forward left and execute a second half turn on the toes as previously described.   Lift the arms overhead and turn on the balls of the feet (see Fig. 4–4).   Complete three dip steps—right, left, right—moving backward instead of forward as previously done (see Fig. 4–6).   **Duck Walk** (Fig. 4–8).   From here, bend both knees until the body is in a squat position with the arms softly out at the sides and take three duck walk steps moving forward—right, left, right.   A duck walk is simply walking forward in this squat position.

SPOTTING.   Hold the near hand.

Fig. 4–8.   Duck walk.

Fig. 4–9.   Knee scale.

9. Knee Scale (Fig. 4–9). From here lean the body forward placing the hands on the beam. The right leg from the foot to the knee is also rested on the beam. Raise the free left leg up behind, straighten the arms, and lift the head. This position is called a knee scale.

10. Fence Dismount (Fig. 4–10). Lower the left leg straight down placing the toe on the beam and extend the right leg back

Fig. 4–10.   Fence dismount.

Fig. 4–10.   Continued.

parallel to the left leg and lift the hips so that the trunk and legs form a straight line (boy's push-up position). Swing the right leg straight down on the right side of the beam, and then swing it back up. Join the other leg to it and dismount on the left side of the beam to a balanced stand with the right hand remaining on the beam for additional support. This is a fence dismount.

SPOTTING. Support the arms at the elbow joints so the arms are straight. Most girls find it difficult to support themselves with a bent arm.

II. LOW INTERMEDIATE ROUTINE IN DETAIL

1. Knee Mount (Fig. 4–11). Facing the side of the beam at the center, take a short run, a two-foot takeoff on the beat board, and land across the beam (perpendicular to the length) on the left knee with both hands on either side of the knee for support. Raise the free right leg behind for a momentary hold.

SPOTTING. The spotter should stand on the opposite side of the beam from the performer to grasp her upper arm or shoulder to prevent her from going too far and falling forward off the beam.

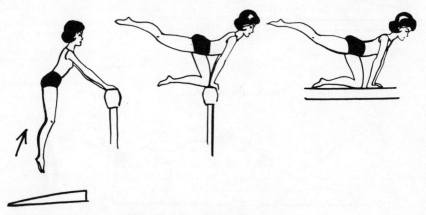

Fig. 4–11. Knee dismount.

2. Swan Balance (Fig. 4–12). Pivot on the left knee a quarter to the left by pulling with the hands and moving to a swan balance. At this point the performer is balanced on the left shin, from the knee to the toe, supported with both hands forward on the beam.

The right leg slides back on the beam until it is straight. For greater stability in balance, the foot in the back may be turned out or perpendicular to the beam. Lift the hands from the beam and straighten the upper trunk until the shoulders and head are in a line directly above the hips; place the arms straight out to the sides at shoulder level.

Fig. 4–12. Swan balance.

3. Take the right foot off the beam and place all the weight on the left shin. Lower the right leg down and forward, and then place the foot on the beam in front of the left knee. Shift the weight to this foot and stand up. Take two backward dip steps starting with the right foot—right, left (see Fig. 4–6). Place the right foot behind and pivot one half to the right (see Fig. 4–4). **Gallop Step** (Fig. 4–13). Take two gallop steps, moving forward with the right leg leading. A gallop step is a step forward in an uneven rhythm. In the weight change from the forward to the back foot, there is a slight hopping motion.

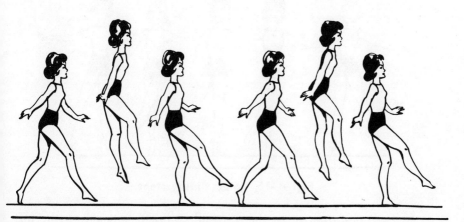

Fig. 4–13. Gallop step.

Fig. 4–14.   Corkscrew turn.

4. Corkscrew Turn (Fig. 4–14).   Then swing the left leg forward and backward.   As it swings backward, make a half turn on the right foot to face the opposite direction.   While turning the left toe circumscribe a circle in the air near the right knee.   Hold the left leg forward in this position for a short balance.   It may be necessary to touch the left foot slightly to the beam for stability and then lift it for a short pose.

5. Place the left foot on the beam and turn a quarter right.   **Side Sliding Steps** (Fig. 4–15).   Take three steps moving sideways to the left (a slide step with no hop).   A more difficult variation is to cross the right foot in front of the left.

Fig. 4–15.   Side sliding steps.

6. Turn one quarter to the left and complete a scale on the left leg with the right leg up behind (see Fig. 4–5).   **Turn in Squat Position** (Fig. 4–16).   Swing the right leg down and bend down to a

Fig. 4–16.   Turn in squat position.

crouch or squat position. Place the right leg on the beam in front
of the left and make a half pivot turn left, in this squat position.
The left leg will now be in front.

7. Move forward until the left shin is on the beam and raise the
right leg up behind to a knee scale (see Fig. 4–9). The hands will
be supporting on the beam. Bring the right leg down and forward
and place the foot on the beam. Stand up and immediately pivot
left on the toes of both feet to face the opposite direction (see Fig.
4–4). Take three forward dip steps to the end of the beam (see
Fig. 4–6). **Straddle Toe Touch Dismount** (Fig. 4–17). Place the
feet side by side on the beam near the end and jump up into the air

Fig. 4–17.   Straddle toe touch dismount.

straddling the legs and piking the hips for a straddle toe touch. Try to touch the toes with the hands. As the ground is approached, bring the legs together and straighten the hips. Land on both feet using a knee bend. Try not to move the feet even one inch after landing.

III. INTERMEDIATE ROUTINE IN DETAIL

1. Half Squat Half Straddle Mount (Fig. 4–18). Facing the side of the beam, take a short run and a two-foot takeoff on the beat board; place the left foot on the beam between the hands with the right leg extended out to the side not touching the beam. Pivot a half left on the left foot bringing the right leg around straight, then bend it, place it on the beam in front of the left foot, and stand.

SPOTTING. Spotting is the same as for the mount in Fig. 4–11.

Fig. 4–18.   Half squat half straddle mount.

2. Take three running steps—left, right, left. Swing the right leg forward and backward and pivot to the right on the left foot (see Fig. 4–14 using opposite feet). **Stag Leap** (Fig. 4–19). Take two more running steps—right, left—to a stag leap. In the stag leap,

Fig. 4–19.   Stag leap.

the right knee bends so that the right toe touches the left knee momentarily before landing on the right foot.

SPOTTING.   Be sure to hold the performer's hand.

3. Execute a front scale on the front leg (see Fig. 4–5). **Cat Walk Step** (Fig. 4–20).   Bring the left leg forward to a step and take two cat walk steps. Jump off the left leg, bend the legs, and bring the knees up toward the chest and then straighten the legs and land on the right leg followed immediately by the left leg. Jump off the left leg again and repeat. It is as though the performer were jumping over a high object by bringing the knees forward and high. The landing is soft and catlike.

Fig. 4–20.   Cat walk step.

Fig. 4–21.   Reverse corkscrew turn.

4. Reverse Corkscrew Turn (Fig. 4–21).   Complete a corkscrew turn which is a pivot on the left foot half left while the extended leg swings forward, bent at the knee.   The foot circumscribes a circle in mid air, passing close to the supporting left knee during this turn.

5. Take two steps—right, left—and on the second step bend down to a squat position and complete a forward roll.   **Forward Head Roll** (Fig. 4–22).   Place the hands on top of the beam, and lift the hips up as high as possible by having the weight on the feet close to the hands.   Turn the head and tuck it under as far as possible, so that the shoulders touch the beam and then push off quickly with the feet.   As the performer rolls, she should change the hands to the bottom of the beam to create a pulling action.   Continue rolling until the back is flat on the beam and the legs are together in a pike position pointing the toes hard towards the ceiling.   Pull hard with the hands on the bottom of the beam; this is a very strong position. If the roll is crooked, simply pull with the hands and arms until the hips are placed on the beam.

Fig. 4–22.   Forward head roll.

Spotting. Support the performer on both sides of the hips to aid in the balance and lift them around if necessary. If more support is needed, step in closer and hold with the shoulder also. Brace the hips until the performer is safely lying on the beam alone. If two spotters are available, they can stand on either side of the performer and support at the hips thus preventing a fall to the side.

6. V-Sit (Fig. 4–23). Keeping the legs off the beam, lift the upper trunk until a v-sit is made. The legs and upper trunk form the letter "V" in this sitting position. In this move, the hand posi-

Fig. 4–23. V-sit.

Photo by Jim Fraser

Dale McClements in a Split on the Balance Beam. (See photo on page 111 for more information about Miss McClements.)

Fig. 4–24.   Scissors jump.

tion on the beam changes from near the neck to the small of the back as the lift to the sitting position is made.

7. Drop the legs, spreading them slightly to pass on either side of the beam, change the hand support to in front of the body, and place the toes back on the beam and come to a stand (see Fig. 4–3). **Scissors Jump** (Fig. 4–24). Step left. Make a scissors jump with the legs passing each other, as in a scissors jump over a high bar in track.   Land first on the right foot and then on the left.

8. Complete two jump changes.   The left foot is forward.   Jump off both feet and bring the right foot forward; jump a second time until the left foot is again forward (see Fig. 4–7). Step forward right on the toes and turn left a half.   The left foot will now be for-

Fig. 4–25.   Body wave.

Fig. 4–24. *Continued.*

ward (see Fig. 4–4). **Body Wave** (Fig. 4–25). Bring the right foot up side by side with the left and the weight evenly distributed on both feet. Execute a body wave. A body wave should feel like a ripple moving up the body. The movement starts by bending both knees and continuing the movement by pulling the hips for-

Photo by Jim Fraser

Spotting the Backward Shoulder Roll on the Balance Beam.

Fig. 4–26.   Step-tap-hops.

ward and upward bending the lower back; then arch the upper back which finally causes the head and arms to whip forward. At the same time, the arms circle counterclockwise beginning at the thigh level continuing backward and upward until the ripple moves out the head. Both arms are extended overhead. This should be performed in one continuous movement to give a flowing impression.

9. Step-Tap-Hops (Fig. 4–26). Complete two step-tap-hops which begin by stepping forward right, bend the left knee until the toe touches the right knee, hop right, and extend the left leg forward. Repeat stepping left, touching the right toe to the left knee and hopping left.

10. Step right and a half turn pivot left. **Backward Shoulder Roll** (Fig. 4–27). Bend the right knee extending the left leg forward until sitting down. Complete a backward shoulder roll. This is performed by lying back on the beam, placing the head to one side of the beam so that the performer rolls over the shoulder. The hand,

Fig. 4–27.   Backward shoulder roll.

Fig. 4–26. *Continued.*

on the same side of the beam as the head, holds the top of the beam; the other hand is on the bottom. Lift both legs up at the same time through a pike position. Round the back when rolling. Land on the shin of one leg, toe pointing back and the other leg extended up. Immediately lift up to a two-hand support with both hands on top of the beam; thus the hand that was on the bottom of the beam will quickly move to the top. Lift up as soon as possible or the balance can be lost at this point. As a general rule, the performer lands on the shin of the leg that is on the same side of the beam as the head— the reason for this being that the weight of the extended straight leg balances the weight of the head on the opposite side. Keep the extended leg over the top of the beam; don't allow it to get off balance out to the side.

SPOTTING. Steady the performer in the prone position by placing your hand on her stomach thus effecting stability. As she rolls and lifts the hips, place your opposite hand under the performer and hold her at the hip. Be prepared to lift on both sides of the hips; use your shoulder for extra lifting power, if needed. As she lifts

Fig. 4–27. *Continued.*

Fig. 4-28.   Full pivot in half squat half straddle position.

her body up, a new steadying position would be to catch the arms until she can hold the balance herself.

11. After the backward roll, the performer is in a position for the knee scale with the balance on the shin of the right leg (see Fig. 4-9). Bend the toes of the right foot under and push backwards until the weight is on the ball of the foot. Bring the left leg down and onto the beam straight behind the body; remain in the squat position and turn one quarter left. This will put the performer in a half squat half straddle position with the weight on the right foot

Fig. 4-29.   Cartwheel dismount off end.

Fig. 4–28. *Continued.*

(see Fig. 4–18). **Full Pivot in Half Squat Half Straddle Position** (Fig. 4–28). Lift the left leg slightly off the beam and then pivot a half right so that the body still is in the half squat half straddle position, facing the opposite direction. Again pivot a half right on the right foot to the original position. Turn one quarter left to face the extended left leg, which is bent and touching the beam. Stand.

12. Cartwheel Dismount Off End (Fig. 4–29). Raise the back leg forward and cartwheel dismount off the end of the beam. This cartwheel differs slightly from the one done on the floor in that,

Fig. 4–29. *Continued.*

when the performer passes through the handstand position, the legs come together and stay together, making a stronger landing position. The hand nearest to the beam may remain on the beam for additional support. The knees should bend on landing. A gymnast should always endeavor to land in balance on a dismount. Steps or hops on landing are considered to be faults.

Photo by Jim Fraser

Doris Fuchs in an English Handstand on the Balance Beam. Doris was the National All-Round Champion in 1961. She is one of the outstanding performers in the world on the uneven parallel bars. Doris was a member of the 1956 and 1960 Olympic teams, the 1959 Pan-American Games team, and the U.S. National teams in 1958, 1961, and 1962. She participated in the World Gymnastic Championships in Moscow in 1958 and in Czechoslovakia in 1962.

Spotting. Practice this on a low beam. The spotter should be standing on the back side of the performer as this stunt is executed. The spotter should be able to grab the hips so that the performer can be directed off the beam. As the beam is raised, spot by reaching up as high as possible, if not at the hips at least on the inside of the rib cage. The spotters other hand should be lending support at the elbow that is nearest the end of the beam. This is the pivoting point of the body through the air. As the performer dismounts, the spotter's supporting hand slips from the elbow of the performer down to the wrist so that she won't fall down or away from her.

IV. LOW ADVANCED ROUTINE IN DETAIL

1. Straddle Mount (Fig. 4–30). Take a run, a two-foot takeoff, land on the top of the beam in a straddle position, with the legs wide apart, while the hands are placed between the legs for support.

Spotting. Spotting is the same as for the mount in Fig. 4–11.

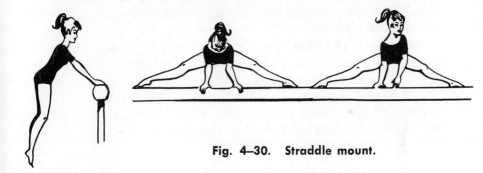

Fig. 4–30. Straddle mount.

2. Free Split (Fig. 4–31). From here it is not difficult to turn one quarter left and go down to free splits without using the hands for balance.

Spotting. Hold the nearer hand.

Fig. 4–31. Free split.

Fig. 4–32. Backward head roll.

3. Bring the back leg down and forward until the performer is sitting on the beam. Then lower the upper body until a lying position is reached. **Backward Head Roll** (Fig. 4–32). Do a backward shoulder roll or a head roll in which the head stays on the beam. The head roll requires a faster start than the backward shoulder roll and a harder lift with the hands to get the head around. Before the roll starts, the hands hold onto the top of the beam directly under the neck and remain on top of the beam all the time. Instead of landing on one shin, as in backward shoulder roll, place the shins of both legs on the beam.

SPOTTING. Hold the hips in the back and be prepared to give a hard lift to get the head around. Refer to the spotting for the backward shoulder roll in Fig. 4–27.

4. Continue into a knee scale (Fig. 4–9). Bring the back leg forward and stand. **Pose** (Fig. 4–33). Place the weight on the left leg and lift the right leg behind momentarily for a pose.

Fig. 4–33. Pose.

Fig. 4–32.   *Continued.*

5. Goose Step (Fig. 4–34).   Three goose steps forward, which is a stiff-legged run—right, left, right—are now completed.

Fig. 4–34.   **Goose step.**

6. Step Behind (Fig. 4–35).   Then, place the left foot ahead of the right foot; however, do it by crossing the left foot behind the

Fig. 4–35.   **Step behind.**

Fig. 4–36. Tuck jump.

right and then forward in front of the right. Step directly forward
—right—and pivot to the right on this same foot. Step left, and hop
left at the same time bending the right knee forward.

7. Next complete two gallop steps forward with the right leg leading (see Fig. 4–3) and bend to a squat position with right leg still
forward. **Tuck Jump** (Fig. 4–36). Jump up high and bend down to
the same squat position. Repeat this movement.

8. Stand, and step forward left and half turn right on toes (see
Fig. 4–4), two step-tap-hops (see Fig. 4–26), and then squat down
in position for a forward roll (see Fig. 4–22). **Straddle Reverse**
(Fig. 4–37). Spread the legs and sit straddling on the beam. Move

Fig. 4–37. Straddle reverse.

Photo by Stuart Hertz

Dale McClements Performing a Split Leap on the Balance Beam. Seattle's seventeen-year-old Dale was Pacific Northwest Senior All-Round Champion in 1960–61–62. She won the Canadian National Senior All-Round Championship in 1961 and the United States National All-Round Championship in 1962. In the summer of 1962 Miss McClements was a member of the U.S. National team that participated in the World Gymnastics Championship in Czechoslovakia.

both hands in front of the body. Swing the legs vigorously backward until the legs and hips are above the beam; the support is forward on the hands. At this point, twist the hips and legs a half turn in the air so that the performer lands straddling the beam and facing the opposite direction.

Fig. 4–38. Split scale.

9. Split Scale (Fig. 4–38). Bend the left knee hard and place the left foot on the beam—pull forward and stand on this leg, step right, and go into a deep scale with the right leg supporting. Make this a split scale if possible with the raised leg in a straight line with the supporting leg. Hold the bottom of the beam.

10. Sissone (Fig. 4–39). Step left into a sissone. The sissone is a ballet movement in which the feet are in fourth position with the right foot forward. Bend both knees and jump slightly forward, landing on the right foot and placing the left foot forward in fourth position. Now jump straight up into the air and bring the right foot forward to fourth again landing on both feet simultaneously. Repeat again.

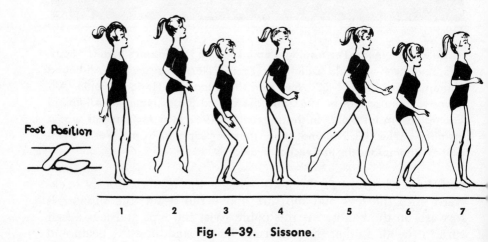

Foot Position

1   2   3   4   5   6   7

Fig. 4–39. Sissone.

Fig. 4–40. English handstand dismount.

11. English Handstand Dismount (Fig. 4–40). Take two steps—left, right—and kick up to a momentary English handstand on the end of the beam. An English handstand is one in which the line of the shoulders is perpendicular to the length of the beam. The hands are held close together with the thumbs touching on the top of the beam and the fingers spread down the sides of the beam. The performer overbalances the handstand and, as she falls beyond the perpendicular line, she executes a quarter twist leaving the left hand on the beam for additional support when landing. The twist could be made in the other direction leaving the right hand on the beam if it can be more easily accomplished to that side.

V. ADVANCED ROUTINE IN DETAIL

1. Forward Roll Mount (Fig. 4–41). Facing the end of the beam, take the customary run, a two-foot takeoff and forward roll to a pike lying position. The hand position differs from the usual hand position in the forward roll on the beam in that the hands are placed on the face side of the head as in a roll in tumbling. After the upper back touches the beam, both hands shift to the bottom of the beam for the strong pulling action.

Fig. 4–41.   Forward roll mount.

SPOTTING.   Lift the hips and then hold behind the hips until the balance is maintained.

2. Lift the upper trunk to a free v-sit without hands to aid the support (see Fig. 4–23).   Bend one knee and place that foot on the beam in front of the body.   Lean forward on that foot and stand. Take three leaping steps to the end of the beam.   Jump down to a squat position, then jump straight up and extend the legs and drop immediately down to a deep squat or bend again (see Fig. 4–34). Come to a stand, swing one leg forward and backward and half turn, put a corkscrew on the last part of the swing.   That is, the free leg when bent forms a circle in the air and passes near to the knee of the other supporting leg after the half turn is completed (see Figs. 4–14 and 4–21).   **Pose** (Fig. 4–42).   Then make a pose by

Fig. 4–42.   Pose.

extending one leg forward and one arm overhead while the other is straight out to the side.

3. Complete two sissones (see Fig. 4-39) and then do a cartwheel. **Cartwheel** (Fig. 4-43). A cartwheel on the beam differs from the one on the floor in several ways: (1) The hands are placed close to the feet on the initial move, (2) the hands should touch the beam at the same time rather than one at a time, (3) the cartwheel is performed quickly, (4) the body is slightly piked at the hip, and (5) the feet are placed close to the hands on regaining the foot balance.

Fig. 4-43. Cartwheel.

Fig. 4-43. *Continued.*

Fig. 4–44. Free sit.

4. Make a full pirouette or turn on one foot. **Free Sit** (Fig. 4–44). Execute a free sit without hands by keeping the hands forward and maintaining balance on one leg as it bends.

5. Complete a backward head roll as explained earlier (see Fig. 4–32). **Pose** (Fig. 4–45). Bring one leg forward and hold this position for a quick pose. This pose is performed by keeping the

Fig. 4–45. Pose.

weight on the back leg, pointing the toes forward, and touching them lightly in front of the body on the beam.

6. Stand and make an immediate half turn by leaving the feet in the same place, but just turning and facing the other direction. Go immediately into a split scale (see Fig. 4–38). **Scissor Handstand** (Fig. 4–46). Place both hands on the beam for an English handstand (see Fig. 4–40) and kick up to a momentary scissor handstand. Kick up with the right leg followed by the left. Stop the right leg when it is over the head and bring it back down to the

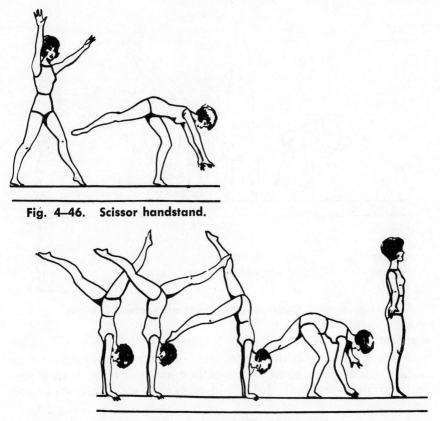

Fig. 4–46.   Scissor handstand.

Fig. 4–46.   Continued.

same place where the kick began; the left leg follows. The legs will scissor or pass each other while the support is on the hands.

7. Immediately slide backward to a free split (see Fig. 4–31). Bring the back leg forward, sit, and then lie back on the beam. **Can-**

Fig. 4–47.   Candle hold.

Fig. 4–48. Cartwheel dismount off center of beam.

dle Hold (Fig. 4–47). Place the hands on the bottom of the beam near the head and lift the rest of the body, through a pike position until the toes point towards the ceiling and the body is in a perfectly straight line from the shoulders to the toes. This is a candle hold.

8. Roll forward, bend one knee, and place that foot on the beam so the performer can stand up. Half turn on the toes. **Cartwheel Dismount Off Center of Beam** (Fig. 4–48). Raise one leg, kick to a cartwheel, putting the legs together for a momentary handstand, and come off on the far or back side of the beam, leaving one hand on the beam for support. This hand will be the one that was first placed on the beam in the cartwheel.

5

Side Horse Vaulting

Most instructional chapters start with the basic movements and proceed step by step to the final product. This chapter will reverse the order by describing the perfected vault. The purpose is to set the goal, with the idea that each vault will lead to a beautiful flying performance. The greater the distance covered, the better the vault.

What are the basics of the perfected vault? Divided into five parts they are: spring, on flight, contact with the horse, after flight, and landing.

The spring is the most important part of the vault, for if the vaulter does not get a strong take off the rest of the vault suffers. It is necessary to carry a long distance and the only source of this power is the run and the takeoff. The approach is not considered part of the vault. However, a long fast run will build up the momentum necessary to carry the performer through the entire vault. The run with no hitch steps or hesitations should build up speed to within a few feet of the takeoff board. Then, with a measured single-foot takeoff the vaulter leaps, swinging the arms in coordination with the pushoff with the takeoff foot. This technique is known as the hurdle. As the vaulter comes down, both feet should contact the board at the point of its greatest spring, which on the Reuther-type board is just in back of the part painted black. This contact is made with the line of the body slightly less than a right angle to the angle of the board (the appearance will be one of leaning back slightly). As the toes contact the board, the ankles bend, then the knees, and then the hips, with the upper body erect. At the same time the arms again swing in line with the body. This position is one of coiled readiness. With a slightly forward lean the whole body is extended in reverse to that of the coil, being sure to take

119

advantage of the natural spring of the board. The most powerful part of the arm swing should come just as the vaulter leaves the board. All this should be timed so that the velocity built up by the run has not been lost.

The "on flight" will be determined by the angle of takeoff—the more powerful the takeoff, the greater height—this should be at least to the horizontal plane and well above the height of the horse. The high carry through the air should be made with the body held in a stretched position with no bend at the hips, the legs straight, and the toes pointed. The head should be up with the eyes focusing on the point of contact with the horse. The arms are in line with the body with no forced reaching.

Contact must be made with the horse; however, this should be momentary and directly on top. Contact on the near side shows lack of flight. The momentary contact indicates the axis of rotation or the changing of position. The contact is not to be used to get into position for the landing. During the contact the elbows must remain straight, the pushoff must be a powerful hand and finger movement.

The "after flight" should be long and be a continuation of all movements preceding it, with the rotation or changing of position performed in a smooth controlled manner.

The landing should be soft and in perfect balance. To achieve the perfectly balanced soft landing, the body must absorb the force by successively bending at the ankles, knees, and hips, with the arms swinging easily down to the sides, then coming to an erect stand.

All these maneuvers should be performed with confidence, precision, and accuracy. Therefore, if precision in the learning process is emphasized so that relearning will not be necessary, confidence will take care of itself.

EQUIPMENT

MATS

Double thickness mats should be placed on the landing side to protect the performer.

TAKEOFF BOARD

The board should be the approved type with resiliency built in and the front part painted with a black stripe to indicate the point of maximum spring.

HORSE

The horse (Fig. 5–1) should be covered with leather or plastic, have a stable base, and have removable pommels. The height should be adjustable. When the pommels are removed, the holes through which the bolts went should be covered with flat pegs (not

Fig. 5–1.   Side horse.

metal) or taped to cover the holes. The dimensions are: length, 1.60 to 1.63 meters or approximately 5 feet 3 inches; width, 35 to 37 centimeters or approximately 14 inches; height from ground, 1.10 meters or approximately 43 inches.

REUTHER-TYPE BOARD

The reuther board (Fig. 5–2) is now the official takeoff board for women's vaulting. It was developed in Germany and is of

Fig. 5–2.   Reuther-type board.

recent origin. It provides more spring than the old fashioned beat board but cannot be classed as a spring board.

SUBSTITUTE OR IMPROVISED EQUIPMENT

SWEDISH BOX

The Swedish Box (Fig. 5–3) is more commonly found in gymnasiums than a regulation horse. This can be built in the workshop. The dimensions are: length, 5 feet 3 inches; width, 14 inches (at top); height, adjustable—3 feet, 3 feet 6 inches, and 4 feet (two removable sections 6 inches each).

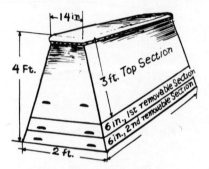

Fig. 5–3.   Swedish box.

As noted by the drawing, spotting will have to be varied slightly because the spotter's near foot will not go under. Leaning against the box and reaching over will work very well.

THE VAULTING TABLE

The vaulting table (Fig. 5–4) can be built very simply. This piece of equipment can be used in the early stages of all vaults. The dimensions are: length, 5 feet 3 inches; width, 4 feet; height, adjustable—2 feet 6 inches to 4 feet.

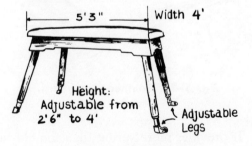

Fig. 5–4.   Vaulting table.

Variations in the height of the table will make it usable in many ways: forward rolls onto the surface, or head and hand springs off it. Its use is only limited by the imagination.

IMPROVISED EQUIPMENT

Mats over lowered parallel bars can be used as a vaulting table.

One enthusiastic gymnastic instructor without a sou in the budget improvised by placing a mat over an old trunk. The trunk was weighted inside to give it stability.

These are just suggestions. With a little ingenuity, some type of equipment can be "made to do."

TERMINOLOGY

The vaults are named by the action, such as the squat vault, or by the part of the body closest to the horse, such as the flank vault, meaning performer's side is closest to the horse as she goes over.

BEGINNER'S PROGRESSION

1. Takeoff Without Board onto Mat. Taking several brisk steps, the performer practices the hurdle and lands on both feet about two and a half feet onto a mat, then recoils and jumps for height and distance. Coordination of all body parts should be stressed (see above).

2. Takeoff with Board onto Mat. As in above, take several steps and hurdle onto the board; at this stage the eyes should be focused on the spot of the takeoff from the board. This should be repeated until the performer is confident that board and body movements are coordinated.

3. Takeoff from Board onto a Vaulting Table. Vaulting onto a table can be used to develop height on the spring. The simple vaults can be started in this way also. For instance, after the spring, jump to a squat position on the table (see page 122).

I. ELEMENTARY VAULTS

The takeoff board should be close to the horse in the early stages of the learning process. Spotting should be done carefully to build confidence in the vaulter.

Precise hand positions should be emphasized. Before trying

any vault, the performer should stand facing the horse and place her hands on the saddle of the horse with the fingers facing forward. From this position, jump to a front rest position with the front of the thighs touching the horse and the back slightly arched. The arms are straight and the shoulders directly over the hands.

Next, to get the feeling of the role the hands and fingers play in vaulting, the performer dismounts backward to the board by pushing strongly upward with fingers and wrist.

1. Squat Vault. The first step is to get the position. The performer stands with hands on the horse; getting a good two-foot take-off, she jumps to a squat position on the horse. The knees are close to the shoulders, the head erect, the soles of feet flat on the horse.

The next step is to develop a good landing. The performer stands erect on the horse, jumps upward and forward from the horse, and absorbs the force by successively bending at the ankles, knees, and hips, with the arms swinging easily down to the sides, then coming to an erect stand. This is called the Courage Dismount.

SPOTTING. During the first step (Fig. 5–5) the spotter stands at the center of the horse facing it, having a forward backward stride with the front foot under the horse. The spotter reaches over

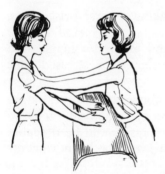

Fig. 5–5.   Spotting the squat vault.

the horse and grasps the performer's arms, with the thumbs in the arm pits and the arms encircled by the index fingers just below the firm muscles of the upper arm (deltoid). In this position the spotter can assist in lifting the performer onto the horse and can control the weight if the performer pitches forward.

During the second step the spotter takes four or five steps backward keeping the forward backward stride. The spotter should focus on the arm pits of the performer and be ready to take short sliding steps forward to grasp the upper arms if the performer loses her balance forward, backward, or sideward.

In the third step the performer takes several brisk steps focusing on the takeoff board going into the hurdle and then focusing on the saddle of the horse making her contact and coming to a squat stand on the horse. Then she pushes off with the hands to a standing dismount.

SPOTTING. The same as for the standing squat mount: reaching over the horse to take hold of the upper arms as the performer pushes up to the squat, taking one or two steps backward with the performer as she dismounts.

The fourth step is to eliminate the squat stand and go all the way through in one motion.

SPOTTING. The spotter takes a position on the landing side of the horse near the croup, with the left side in contact with the horse, with a side stride position elongated in the direction of the force. As the performer nears the horse, she concentrates on the right arm. As the performer takes off the board, she grasps the right wrist with the left hand and the upper arm with the right, with the thumb on the outside of the arm. As the performer clears the horse, she lets go of the upper arm but continues to hold onto the wrist until the performer is under control. This means that the spotter must move with the performer.

Contact with the performer can be eliminated as soon as the vault is done with ease, but the spotter should always be in position and alert.

As soon as the performer has confidence in her ability on any of the elementary vaults, she should work on a longer run and should move the takeoff board back away from the horse. After the preliminary steps, the performer should work for a strong pushoff with the hands and a landing well away from the horse on the off flight.

2. Flank Vault. In the first step in the learning process, the takeoff board should be placed toward one end of the horse to allow enough space for a stationary position on the horse. The performer should execute a standing takeoff from the board and come to a side leaning support on the top of the horse. The feet should be together and the legs extended with the side of one foot resting on the horse. The top hand should be removed from the horse as soon as the performer reaches the side leaning support. In order to dismount, the legs are swung forward and the body remains facing forward.

SPOTTING. (Fig. 5–6). The spotter stands on the landing side of the horse on the side of the performer's supporting hand. Grasp the wrist with the hand which is away from the horse and grasp the upper arm of the performer with the hand which is closest to the horse.

Fig. 5–6. Spotting the flank vault.

As soon as the elementary form is mastered, the takeoff board should be replaced at the center of the horse. The takeoff must be with both feet simultaneously and the contact with the saddle is made with both hands. As soon as the feet are airborne the legs swing to the side and the top arm is removed from the horse. The body should remain facing forward and the shoulders should be directly over the supporting hand.

SPOTTING. The spotter stands on the landing side of the horse on either the neck or croup end, depending on the performer's supporting arm. The spotting is the same as for the stationary side leaning position.

3. Face Vault or Front Vault. This vault may be started in the same manner as the Flank Vault by taking a front leaning position on the horse with the top of the toes resting on the top of the horse, then swinging down to a landing.

Both hands are placed on the top of the horse with the fingers pointing the long way of the horse. The performer takes off with both feet, places the hands on the horse, and swings over the horse facing it. The landing is made with the side toward the apparatus.

SPOTTING. Spotting is the same as the Flank Vault.

4. Wolf Vault or Half Squat Half Straddle. The learning process of this vault is similar to that of the other vaults. The performer starts with a resting position on the saddle, one leg in squat position and the other in a side extended position on the croup. The dismount is accomplished by jumping forward to a landing position, being sure that the supporting hand on the straddle side is removed with the first movement (cutoff).

For the vault over, the performer takes a double take off, then places her hands on the saddle, keeping the head high, the squat leg is brought into a tight tuck with the leg perpendicular to the horse and directly over the saddle. The straddle leg is extended to the side with the side of the foot toward the horse, leg straight and toes extended.

SPOTTING. The spotter supports the arm on the squat side as in the Flank Vault.

5. Straddle Vault. The first step in learning this vault is to practice on the floor to get a wide straddle position. The position may need to be preceded with some stretching exercises on the floor or at the barre. The performer should be able to touch the floor with the hands directly under the hips. Leap frog is another leadup.

The vault is again started with the position on the horse. The legs should be resting on each end of the horse in a wide side stride. The legs should be straight, the hands resting on the saddle, the hips well above the shoulders, and the head in line with the upper body. Getting a good push off with the hands, the performer jumps high off the horse to a good soft landing.

After the preliminary practice it is an easy matter to clear the horse. The hips should be brought into a sharp pike just as the hands touch the horse, then with a strong finger and wrist push, the legs pass outside the hands. The landing is made by snapping the legs to a good standing position.

SPOTTING. On the stand position, the spotter stands in front of the performer in the same position as the first phase of the Squat Vault. On the running vault, the same technique is used as that in the Courage Dismount.

6. Thief or Window Vault. This is the only vault which does not require a two-foot takeoff. It is performed by taking a long step and extending the leading leg over the horse, then bringing the takeoff foot to meet it before the hands touch the horse. The Thief can be practiced on a vaulting table by taking a long step and coming to a long sitting position on the table, placing the hands on the table just before coming to the sitting position (to absorb the force) (Fig. 5–8, page 132).

SPOTTING. Same as the Flank Vault.

Having learned the elementary vaults, the performer should work on adding distance to the "on flight," a good distance on the "off flight," and add variations to each vault.

The takeoff board should be moved away from the horse by gradual stages. Whenever the board is moved, the distance to the starting point of the run should be paced off by the vaulter. This starting point should be marked by a small piece of tape or a chalk line. The takeoff for the hurdle should also be marked so that the vaulter will hit the board at the point of maximum lift. As the distance of the "on flight" becomes greater, the force built up by the run needs to be increased. This should be a brisk run, but at the same time a controlled one.

The increase of the force will lead to greater distance on the "off flight" if the hands touch the horse for a very short time. This needs to be practiced by doing the elementary vaults and paying particular attention to the finger and wrist push.

The Courage Dismount can be used to develop a straight body descent. The performer should stand on the horse and, with a good spring and a strong arm swing, jump high into the air and well away from the horse. The position of the body should be a perpendicular layout position with the arms just above shoulder height and a slight arch in the back. The landing should be soft and well controlled.

To add variations to the vaults already learned, the performer can combine two vaults. As an example, just as the body goes over the horse in the front vault, one hand can be thrown up and a quarter turn executed so that the performer lands with the side to the horse, facing the opposite direction as she would for a Flank Vault. Such variations add interest and develop consciousness of body position.

II. INTERMEDIATE VAULTS

1. Stoop Vault.   The first in this series should be the Stoop Vault. The stoop position is one in which the legs are held straight and together directly under the body in a pike position (Fig. 5–10, page 132).

The first step is to practice the position on the floor. With the feet together and flat on the floor the performer reaches down with the hands and places the palms flat on the floor. After this is accomplished, the legs should be brought forward inside the arms by getting a good push from the floor with the wrists and fingers.

Another step could be to take off and land in a stoop position on a broad surface at a lesser height than the horse. This could be a vaulting table or an improvised surface, so long as it is stable.

After confidence has been built up, the vaulter goes back to the horse and does the vault.

Spotting. Two spotters should be used. One on the takeoff side to boost the hips if needed. The second stands on the landing side, either at the side as in the Squat Vault or in front as in the Straddle Vault.

2. Head Spring—Pike Position.   The vaulter should perfect the head spring on the mats before starting this vault (see Chapter 2). Unlike other vaults in which the head is held in line with the body, it is necessary to get the head down and the hips up. The vaulter will have some feeling of this hip lift in both the Straddle and the Stoop Vault.

In the elementary phase, the board should be place close to the horse. Standing with the hands supported on the saddle of the horse and a bit more than shoulder distance apart, the performer jumps, bringing the hips into a high pike position being sure that the legs are straight and coming back to a landing position on the take off side. Next, the performer does the jump, but this time places the top of the head on the top of the horse.

Next, with support from the spotters, the performer comes to a pike head stand on the horse. After a thorough orientation to this position, she lets the hips go slightly past the shoulders. Then with the legs snapping in the rotary movement—up, out, and then down— she completes the movements necessary for the spring and the vault.

With a few preliminary steps, the performer should take off from the board and go through the vault. The takeoff board should be placed far enough from the horse to get momentum to carry the vaulter through the vault.

SPOTTING. On the hold phase, as well as the full vault, one spotter stands on the landing side with the left side leaning against the apparatus, with the left foot under it. The right leg is in an elongated side stride position. The right hand is placed under the near shoulder with the thumb on the back and the palm under the shoulder, with the fingers pointing toward the chest. The left hand should grasp the wrist of the near arm. As the snap is made, the first spotter lifts the shoulder and releases this hand, continues to hold the wrist with the left hand, and moves with the performer if she goes forward. The second spotter stands on the takeoff side and, if the performer needs help, the spotter lifts the legs to help in getting the rotary movement.

III. ADVANCED VAULTS

1. Hand Spring—Pike Body Ascent. The initial step here can be practiced with a spring board or a mini tramp. This is used only until the vaulter masters the handspring position. The board or mini tramp should not be used for the vault because it does not have the correct angle for takeoff.

The hand stand need be only a three quarter stand, for, as the pushoff is made, the momentum built up by the run and the whip of the legs will carry the body over. The arms must be straight in the handspring. On the dismount the back should not be overly arched and the legs should be snapped down to get the feet under for the landing.

SPOTTING. On this practice, the same spotting is used as for the headspring. On the dismount it may be necessary to transfer the right hand to a position under the shoulder blades to give support if the vaulter loses balance backwards.

Before actually making the running vault, the vaulter should practice the approach and hurdle. The hurdle should be longer and lower than in diving. The height does not come from the board so much as from the momentum built up by the run and the spring of the body. The hurdle is more an extension of the run than it is a separate technique.

A long free flight to the horse makes it easier for the body to carry over in the handspring. Taking off too close to the horse cramps the arms and the elbows bend. The handspring must be done with the arms straight. The following discussion on straight body ascents will help in getting the feeling of the "on flight," although the handspring can be done in a pike position on the "on flight."

2. Hand Spring—Straight Body Ascent (Fig. 5–7). The Handspring is the beginning of the more advanced vaults. Although the Squat, Straddle, and Stoop can be done with a straight body ascent, the Handspring lends itself to practice a little more easily.

On the straight body ascent the body must be above the horizontal and well above the horse. There should be no bend at the hips after takeoff, and, depending upon the vault, the body should remain in a fully extended position until a change of position is made or the legs are snapped to the landing. If the vault is to be a straddle, the

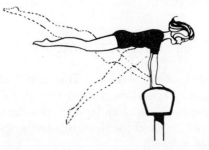

Fig. 5–7. Hand spring—straight body ascent.

body is straight until the hands touch the horse, at which time the legs are separated and the legs brought outside the arms. In other vaults, such as the Handspring, the body remains straight until the landing is made.

Practice methods for the straight body ascent are started gradually by easy steps leading up to the full speed necessary to carry the performer through the vault. In these steps, the performer and the spotter, or spotters, are a team.

SPOTTING. The main spotter (or spotters) stand on the takeoff side. The other spotter stands on the landing side.

The takeoff board is placed back far enough so the vaulter will have to jump before placing the hands on the horse. First from a stand, the vaulter takes off upward and forward, reaching out with the hands toward the horse. When the performer's hands touch the horse, the main spotter lifts the legs into a position above the horizontal, then lets her down gently on the same side of the horse.

The next step is the same except the vaulter takes a short run. Emphasis here should be placed on the angle of the arms. As the vaulter takes off, the body goes high into the air and the arms reach down for the horse at an angle of about forty-five degrees.

From a short run the vaulter repeats the above and goes up into the hand stand.

A longer measured run will give the momentum to carry the vaulter over in the hand stand position. It is the force of the run which is momentarily stopped by the contact with the horse which lifts the hips above the horizontal.

Variations and combinations are illustrated in the *Amateur Athletic Union's Guide* in the Table of Vaults and Evaluation.

Swan Series. The last in the progression of vaults is known as the Swan Series. These are the ones in which the body is held in extended position throughout the vault, with just a momentary touching of the horse on the flight over it.

Fig. 5–8.   Thief or window vault.   Rating: 7.0.

Fig. 5–9.   Flank vault.   Rating: 7.0.

Fig. 5–10.   Bent hip ascent, stoop vault.   Rating: 7.0.

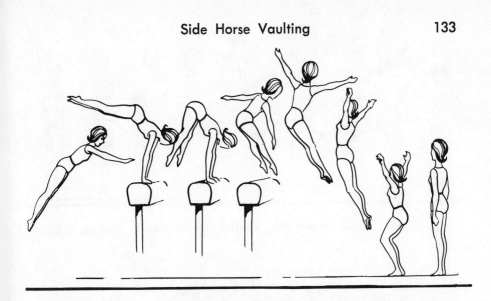

Fig. 5–11.   Bent hip straddle, vault with half turn.   Rating: 8.0.

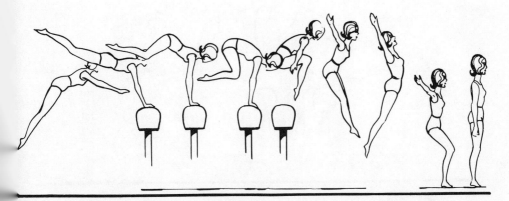

Fig. 5–12.   Straight body ascent, squat vault.   Rating: 8.5.

Fig. 5–13. Flank/front vault, quarter turn outward. Rating: 8.5.

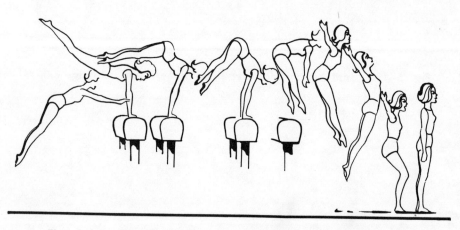

Fig. 5–14. Straight body ascent, straddle vault. Rating: 10.0.

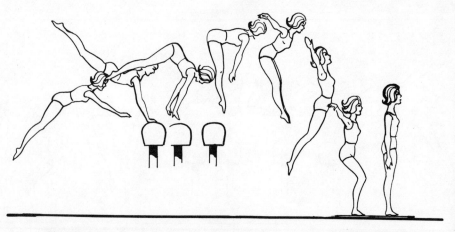

Fig. 5–15. Straight body ascent, stoop vault. Rating: 10.0.

Fig. 5–16. Straight body ascent, handstand quarter turn. Rating: 10.0.

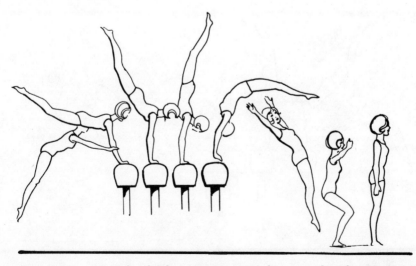

Fig. 5–17. Straight body ascent, straight arm handspring. Rating: 10.0.

Fig. 5–18. Straight body ascent, handstand quarter turn pivot cart-wheel. Rating: 10.0.

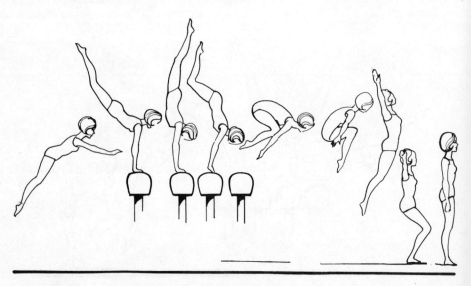

Fig. 5–19. Straight body ascent, handstand squat vault. Rating: 10.0.

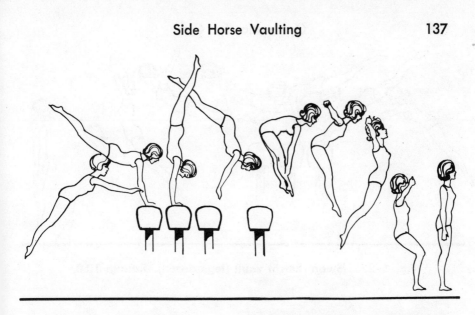

Fig. 5–20.   Straight body ascent, handstand straddle vault.   Rating: 10.0.

Fig. 5–21.   Straight body ascent, handstand stoop vault.   Rating: 10.0.

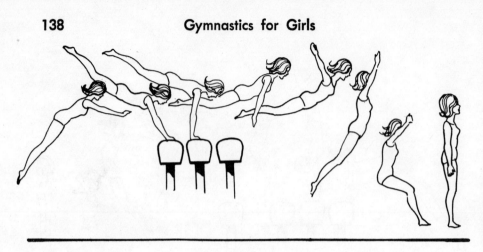

Fig. 5–22.   Swan (hetch) vault (legs closed).   Rating: 10.0.

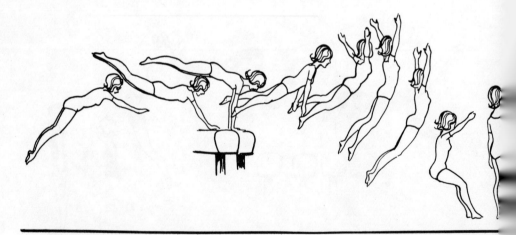

Fig. 5–23.   Straight body ascent, straight hip straddle vault (swan, legs straddled).   Rating: 10.0.

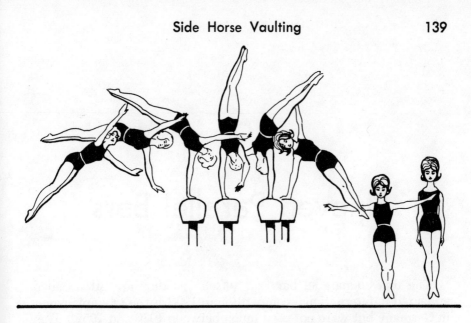

Fig. 5–24. Straight body ascent, cartwheel. Rating: 10.0.

6

Uneven Parallel Bars

The uneven parallel bars, or "offsets" as they are often called, appeared in international competition in 1936 at the Olympic games in Germany but were not used much between 1936 and 1952. They were used again in the 1952 Olympics and have since been a standard piece of equipment in all women's gymnastic competition. The uneven bar event is probably the most spectacular women's event.

Because the offset bars do not require the strength necessary for even parallel bar participation, they allow girls a much wider range of stunts, and combinations of stunts, than are possible on the bars of equal height that are used by men. The uneven parallel bars are merely two horizontal bars, one two and a half feet above and approximately a foot and a half to the side of the other, but they are easier on the hands and softer to land on than the steel horizontal bars used by men because they are larger in diameter and have more "flex" or spring.

VALUES

In most girl's gymnastic events the lower body is used primarily, but the offset bars require considerable upper body development. Although such stunts as kips, hip circles, and long hangs are not in themselves strength work, the bars do require more shoulder, arm, and abdominal usage than girls are normally accustomed to. Many girls who do not have the ballet and modern dance background or the natural grace and flexibility found almost essential for some girl's gymnastic events find they can compete on equal terms on the offset bars because this apparatus requires strength, balance, timing, and courage rather than grace and elasticity.

RULES

Because the event is so new the rules are still in a process of being revised and modified regularly. At present, exercises should be composed primarily of swinging movements and vaults in which one or both hands momentarily release the bars. Skills that involve suspension rather than support should predominate. Supports are utilized only as temporary positions. Movements common in other events should be avoided on the uneven bars. Balances are acceptable provided they are specially suited to the bars and not commonly used in floor exercises or balance beam. As in all women's events, stunts that primarily require strength rather than skill should not be used. To perform well on the uneven parallel bars a girl must possess considerable strength, but she should not select stunts for her routine that force her to display masculine-type strength. The stunts should flow smoothly and should require an equal use of both the high and low bars. Only vaults and swings requiring a hand grasp are considered to be real "difficulties" on the uneven bars. Dismounts are not accepted as "difficulties" unless they require a hand grip. An exercise should be composed of at least ten parts. It should start with a mount from the floor or beat board to the apparatus and terminate with a dismount from the apparatus to the floor. The performer must land in balance in a stationary standing position. Any fall off the uneven bars is penalized by a one-point deduction from the score, provided the contestant remounts and continues her exercise immediately. If the interruption lasts more than three seconds, the exercise will be considered ended. Compulsory exercises may be repeated in their entirety, at the discretion of the contestant, if the judges are notified before a score is given. In this case only the second exercise is scored.

TEACHING SUGGESTIONS

As was stated in Chapter 1, unless a class is extremely small, the uneven parallel bars will have to be used in conjunction with other gymnastic equipment in a physical education class. The boys' horizontal bar, especially if it is adjustable and can be lowered, can be used to teach many uneven parallel bar skills. Because of the smaller diameter of the bar, many skills are easier on the horizontal bar. The boys' parallel bars, with one bar removed, can also be used as an extra piece of equipment for practice of low-bar stunts. While waiting for their turn to perform or spot, girls assigned to the offset bars should be instructed to practice floor exercise or balance beam skills adjacent to the bars. Whenever possible, two girls should work on the bars at the same time so as to get maximum use out of the piece of equipment. There is ample room between the uprights for two performers to execute many of the basic skills on both the high and low bars.

Most girls grip the bar with their thumbs on the same side of the bar as their fingers for almost all stunts performed. In handstands the thumbs are normally placed on the opposite side of the bar from the fingers. These are the two general rules for thumb placement but are not hard and fast rules. Many good performers wrap their thumbs around the bar for other stunts as well as handstands. The size of the hand is somewhat of a factor in deciding whether to use the thumbs or not. Girls with small hands find it difficult to wrap their thumbs around the bar.

SAFETY PRECAUTIONS

Most of the safety precautions listed in Chapter 1 apply to the uneven parallel bars. Only those that are particularly important are repeated here:

1. Check equipment to see that adjustments are tight, bars are not cracked, and rollers are released (if old type bars are being used).

2. Place mats for adequate protection. If only one girl is working on the bars at a time the mat placement shown in Fig. 6–1a provides adequate protection, but if plenty of mats are available,

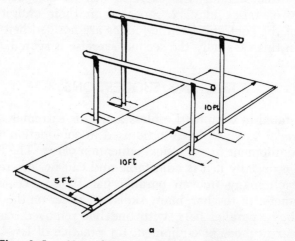

a

Fig. 6–1. Mat placement for uneven parallel bars.

they should be placed as shown in Fig. 6–1b. If two girls are work-ing on the bars at the same time, the second arrangement will have to be used. Extra mats should be moved into position for the practice of certain stunts. It is desirable to have a specially fitted mat underneath the bars. These can be obtained from the manu-facturer. Be sure that mats are not overlapped, creating a dangerous uneven landing surface.

3. Teach stunts on the low bar whenever possible, rather than the high bar, or on the low horizontal bar, where the spotters can assist easily. Make sure all students learn how to spot. Use two or more spotters when one is insufficient to provide adequate protection. Warn spotters about the possibility of injury to themselves if their arm is caught above the bars and the weight of the performer should fall on it.

4. Provide gymnastic chalk for performers to use on their hands to minimize slipping.

OTHER SOURCES OF INFORMATION

Because this is such a new event, there is very little written material available. A considerable number of stunts are described in this chapter, but there are many other excellent skills on the uneven bars that are not included. The most complete source for additional stunts is a book by Walter J. Lienert, *The Modern Girl Gymnast on the Uneven Parallel Bars* (see Bibliography). Women should also read the horizontal bar chapter in books on men's gym-

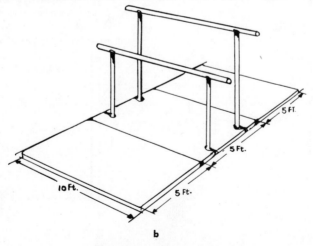

b

Fig. 6–1. *Continued.*

nastics because many of the stunts that can be done on the horizontal bar can also be done on the uneven parallel bars.

CONVERTING "OLD-STYLE" EVEN BARS TO UNEVEN BARS

The old style of men's parallel bars can be converted into offset bars by the use of four steel tubes. Two tubes are required for each upright support of the bar to be raised. Insert one tube into each vertical support, the top protruding out of the top of the support at least a foot. The second two tubes must be of larger diameter permitting them to fit over the inserted tubes and rest on the top of the upright posts. The length of these second two tubes should be about two and one half feet. The original shafts that are attached to the wooden top rail fit into the second two tubes (see Fig. 6–2a).

Another method of converting even bars to uneven bars is to have two longer vertical shafts made that can be exchanged for the two regular length shafts on one of the wooden top rails. Remove the pins that connect the wooden top rail to the two regular shafts and substitute a nut and bolt permitting the use of either the long or regular vertical shafts (see Fig. 6–2b).

Whichever method is used, holes can be drilled for the pins so that the high bar can be set at the proper height of 2300 mm. (or approximately 7 feet 6 inches). The low bar should be set at

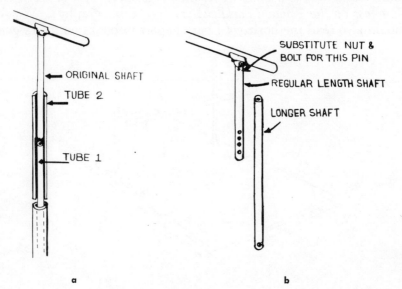

Fig. 6–2.

1500 mm. (or approximately 5 feet). The distance between the bars may vary from 430 to 480 mm. (or approximately 16½ inches to 18 inches).

ABBREVIATED ROUTINE DESCRIPTIONS

I. 1. Stand facing low bar underneath high bar, jump to front support on low bar.
    2. Swing left leg over low bar to crotch support.
    3. Half turn in crotch support.
    4. Forward knee circle.
    5. Swing left leg over low bar to sitting position.
    6. Drop to a hang on high bar with a half turn.
    7. Place feet on low bar and slide over to a sitting position.
    8. Turn to front support on low bar.
    9. Dismount backward by casting away from the bar to a stand facing the bars.

II. 1. Stand under high bar facing low bar, jump to a hang on high bar, raise legs sideways over low bar, and rest them on the bar.
    2. Kick-rise to front support on high bar.
    3. Swan balance on high bar.
    4. Circle backward extending one leg forward to a crotch support on low bar.
    5. Swing forward leg back to a front support.
    6. Backward hip circle.
    7. Squat dismount to a stand with the back to the bars.

III. 1. Stand facing low bar and high bar, single leg swing up on low bar to crotch support.
    2. Backward crotch circle.
    3. Swing back leg over to sitting position on low bar facing high bar.
    4. Lower to hang on high bar with a half turn.
    5. Straddle legs up and over low bar, bounce back of thighs on bar, and hip-swing up to front support on high bar.
    6. Roll forward over high bar and immediately bounce from back of legs with half turn to crotch position.
    7. Swing back leg over low bar to a sitting position.
    8. Lower to hang on high bar.
    9. Skin-the-cat, roll-turn to one leg squat on low bar.
    10. Stand and swing left leg up and over high bar and back to a stand on low bar.
    11. Underswing dismount from high bar to a stand with the back to the bars.

IV. 1. Jump to a one-legged squat stand on low bar and grasp high bar with immediate half-turn.

2. Kick-rise to front support on high bar.
3. Forward hip circle.
4. Cast back to hang and swing to hip circle on low bar.
5. Squat through with left leg.
6. Crotch circle forward with regrasp of high bar.
7. Swing right leg over to outer seat on low bar, hands on high bar.
8. Place feet on low bar, arch up to stand, and half turn to face high bar.
9. Backward sole circle on low bar with cast to regrasp high bar.
10. Skin-the-cat and roll-turn to one leg squat on low bar.
11. Kick up to momentary handstand with one hand on low bar and one hand on high bar, drop legs over high bar to front support position.
12. Roll forward and grasp low bar, cast off from the stomach on high bar to handstand on low bar with a quarter-turn dismount to stand.

V. 1. Stand underneath high bar with regular grip on low bar, glide-kip to front support.
2. Backward hip circle.
3. Squat feet up on low bar and stand shifting hands to high bar.
4. Shoot to dislocate on high bar and swing to hip circle on low bar.
5. Eagle back to hang on high bar.
6. Place feet on low bar and stand.
7. Straddle-jump backward over high bar with regrasp and swing to a hip circle on low bar.
8. Cast backward with a half turn to a squat stand on low bar facing high bar.
9. Sole circle and cast to hang on high bar with a half turn.
10. Stomach whip on low bar, place feet on low bar, and kick to front support on high bar.
11. Squat through to stand on low bar.
12. Jump backward over high bar to an inverted pike hang on high bar and straddle cutoff dismount forward to a stand facing the bars.

I. BEGINNING ROUTINE IN DETAIL

1. Jump to Front Support (Fig. 6–3). The performer stands underneath the high bar facing the low bar and grasps the low bar in a regular or overgrip with the hands about a shoulder width apart (1). She then jumps upward, presses down with the arms, and leans

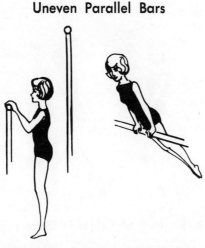

Fig. 6–3. Jump to front support.

forward so that the upper thighs rest against the bar with the body slightly arched. The arms should be straight with part of the weight supported by the arms and part rested against the bar. If the gymnast leans well forward, most of the weight will rest on the bar. This position is called a front support (2).

SPOTTING. The spotter stands between the bars with her right side against the low bar. The right hand is placed on the upper arm of the performer to prevent her from jumping too far over the bar. The left hand gives her a boost under the buttocks if needed.

2. Swing Left Leg from Front Support to Crotch Support (Fig. 6–4). The left leg is raised sideways and swung over the bar to a crotch support. Most of the weight should be shifted to the right hand during this movement. The right arm should be kept straight. The left hand releases the bar as the leg passes over and then regrasps in the same position (1).

1

Fig. 6–4. Swing left leg from front support to crotch support.

Fig. 6–5.   Half turn right in crotch support.

SPOTTING.   The spotter stands in front of the bar on the right side of the performer and holds her right arm to give her a sense of security and to make sure that she maintains balance.

3. Half Turn Right in Crotch Support (Fig. 6–5).   From the crotch support, most of the weight is shifted to the left hand while the right hand reaches backward and grasps the high bar in a regular grip.   The head and upper body should turn to the right during this movement so that the performer can see the high bar (1).   The left hand can now release the bar, reach over the left leg, and grasp the low bar again on the other side of the left leg in a reverse grip. The lower body completes the half turn during this hand motion so that the performer is in a crotch support position facing the high bar with the right leg forward, the left hand on the low bar, and the right hand on the high bar (2).

SPOTTING.   The spotter holds the performer's left arm during the right hand shift to give her a sense of security and make sure that she maintains balance.   After the previous stunt the spotter must quickly step around the performer to reposition herself to spot this stunt.

4. Forward Knee Circle (Fig. 6–6).   The right hand is removed from the high bar and regrasps the low bar in a reverse grip (the left hand is already in a reverse grip).   It is very important that both hands are in a reverse grip for the forward knee circle as the performer can easily fall off the bar if a regular grip is used.   To start the forward knee circle the hips are raised upward and backward so that the weight is supported on the hands.   The right leg is bent and the bar is hooked in the bend of the leg (1).   The performer falls forward with the arms perfectly straight, keeping the radius of the circle as long as possible.   The head must stay in line with

Fig. 6–6.   Forward knee circle.

the body during the fall forward (2). The two common mistakes during the fall forward are dropping the chin onto the chest and bending the arms. Both of these faults shorten the radius of the circle. As soon as the head passes under the bar the radius can be shortened to facilitate the return to the top of the bar. This is done by dropping the chin onto the chest and bending the arms (3). As the circle is completed, the head should be raised again to look for the high bar and the right arm should release the low bar and reach for the high bar with a regular grip (4).

SPOTTING. The spotters (two) stand on the outside of the low bar with their side against the bar. They reach under the bar with the near arm and grasp the near wrist of the performer in a regular grip. This gives the performer confidence and, if she should fall off, the spotters, by lifting on her wrist, can keep her head and upper body from hitting the mat. As the performer passes under the bar and starts the upward part of circle the spotters can lift under the performer's back with their free hand. During the latter stage of the circle the hand that was on the performer's wrist can release the wrist and be used to pull down on the performer's straight leg to assist her back to the top of the bar. The spotters can also stop the performer from falling forward into a second circle by grasping the performer's straight leg as the circle is completed.

5. Swing Left Leg from Crotch Support to Inner Seat (Fig. 6–7). The weight is shifted to the right arm and the left leg is raised up and over the low bar to finish in a sitting position on the low bar. The left hand has to release the low bar as the leg passes over. Instead

1

Fig. 6–7.   Swing left leg from crotch support to inner seat.

of replacing the left hand on the low bar, it immediately reaches for the high bar and grasps in a reverse grip (1). The hands are now in a mixed grip on the high bar—the right in a regular or overgrip, the left in a reverse or undergrip.

SPOTTING. Spotting is not really necessary for this stunt, but the spotter should stand between the bars on the performer's right side to give her confidence.

6. Drop to Hang on High Bar and Turn Right to Face Low Bar (Fig. 6–8). If the performer leans forward slightly from the sitting position and lowers the legs, the buttocks will slide off the bar. There will be a slight forward swing in the hanging position (1). As soon as the weight is entirely on the hands, the right hand is released to start the turn in a backward direction. The performer looks up toward the bar, turns the head and upper body to the right (2), and regrasps the bar again as soon as possible in a regular grip. After

1   2   3

Fig. 6–8.   Drop to hang on high bar and turn right to face low bar.

the half turn has been completed, the left hand, which was originally in a reverse grip, will be in a regular grip (3).

Spotting. The spotter stands beside the performer with one hand on her abdomen and one hand on her lower back. As the performer slides off the bar, the spotter takes some of her weight, helps her through the turn, and makes sure she lands on her feet if she loses her grasp on the bar.

Teaching Technique. The first few times that the performer tries this stunt the turn should not be attempted. After the hanging position is reached and the swing has been stopped by the spotter, the turn can be tried in a dead hang or stationary position.

7. Raise Legs to Sitting Position on Low Bar (Fig. 6–9). If the half turn is done correctly, there will be a slight swing in the hanging position back toward the low bar. At this time the legs should be raised in a tuck and the feet placed on the low bar (1). The feet then slide over the bar to an outer seat. The hands remain on the high bar (2).

Spotting. The spotter stands beside the performer with one hand under the back and one under the thighs. Some girls might need help in raising the legs to place the feet on the bar.

1   2

Fig. 6–9. Raise legs to sitting position on low bar.

8. Turn to Front Support (Fig. 6–10). The left hand is shifted to a reverse grip on the low bar very close to the left thigh. The performer leans to the left and then turns to the left (1). At the same time the high bar is released by the right hand and, as the half turn is completed, the right hand grasps the low bar in a regular grip. The turn is actually a roll on the thigh of the left leg over the left

1   2

Fig. 6–10. Turn to front support.

hand and ends in a front support on the low bar facing the high bar (2). The upper body must lean back at the start of the turn and forward as the turn is completed or there will be a tendency to lose balance and slide off the outer side of the bar.

SPOTTING. The spotter stands between the bars on the performer's right side as she starts the turn and reaches under her back and grasps her left arm with one hand to prevent her from falling off. The other hand is used to push under the performer's right hip to help her execute the turn.

   9. Cast Off Backward to a Stand Facing the Bars (Fig. 6–11). From the front support position the arms are bent slightly so that the lower

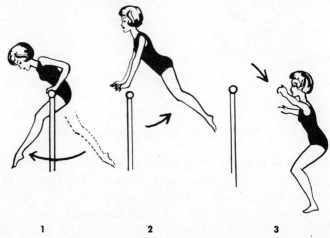

1   2   3

Fig. 6–11. Cast off backward to a stand facing the bars.

abdomen, rather than the upper thighs, rests against the bar. From this position the legs are swung rapidly under the bar so that the body is in a pike position (1). The direction of the legs is reversed and they are swung hard upward and away from the bar. At the same time the arms push away from the bar (2). The bar is released and the performer dismounts to a stand facing the bars. The landing should be in balance with the legs bent and the arms out to the side slightly above the shoulders (3).

SPOTTING. The spotter stands beside the performer with one hand on her arm and one hand on her lower thigh. The hand on the thigh helps in the forward motion of the thigh and then lifts under the thigh during the upward and backward motion. The hand on the arm is used to make sure the performer's arms do not collapse as the push-away is started. A collapse of the arms could result in the upper body or face dropping against the bar. The holding of the arm also aids the performer in maintaining balance on the dismount.

II. LOW INTERMEDIATE ROUTINE IN DETAIL

1. Jump to Hang on High Bar, Raise Legs Sideways over the Low Bar, and Rest the Legs on the Bar (Fig. 6–12). The performer stands under the high bar facing the low bar and jumps to a hang with a regular grip on the high bar (1). The legs are raised sideward, upward, and then forward (2). They are then lowered so that the backs of the thighs rest on the low bar (3).

SPOTTING. The spotter stands on the right side of the performer with one hand on the small of her back and one hand under her

1   2   3

Fig. 6–12. Jump to hang on high bar, raise legs sideways over the low bar, and rest the legs on the bar.

1 **2** **3**

Fig. 6–13. Kick-rise to front support on high bar.

lower thighs. Some girls will have considerable difficulty raising the legs and will have to be aided by the spotter.

TEACHING TECHNIQUES. Girls who have extremely weak abdominal muscles should first practice raising the legs with bent knees.

2. Kick-Rise to Front Support on High Bar (Fig. 6–13). From the hanging position, with the back of the legs resting on the low bar, the left leg is bent and the foot is placed on the bar. The right leg is kept straight and raised so that the ankle is close to the high bar (1). The right leg is then swung vigorously downward and at the same time the left leg is straightened by pushing off the low bar (2). The arms pull upward and then press downward until the front support position is reached (3).

SPOTTING. The spotter stands on the bent leg side of the performer and pushes under her buttocks and then controls any forward movement over the high bar by grasping the ankle.

3. Swan Balance (Fig. 6–14). In the front support position the performer places the bar at the hips, which are usually the balance

Fig. 6–14. Swan balance.

point of the body, and then leans forward and raises the feet to an arched position. The hands release the bar and are placed straight out to the sides.

SPOTTING. A tall spotter can reach up high with one hand and be ready to take weight on the chest in case the performer overbalances. Shorter spotters can stand on the low bar, lean against the high bar for stability, and spot from this position.

TEACHING TECHNIQUE. Teach the stunt first on the low bar where the performer will have more confidence and the spotters can help more readily.

4. Partial Circle Backward and Extend Legs to a Crotch Support on Low Bar (Fig. 6–15). The high bar is regrasped in a regular grip and the performer returns to the front support position by raising the upper body and lowering the legs. This backward circling movement is continued by raising the legs forward and leaning the upper body backward. The legs are scissored slightly with the left leg forward and the right leg back as the performer drops away from the high bar (1) to a hanging position. The left leg shoots forward over the low bar so that the back of the left thigh comes to rest on the bar. One hand at a time is shifted to the low bar (2) and as this is done the weight is also shifted forward to a crotch support position (3).

SPOTTING. The spotter stands underneath the high bar to the side of the performer. As the performer leans backward, one hand

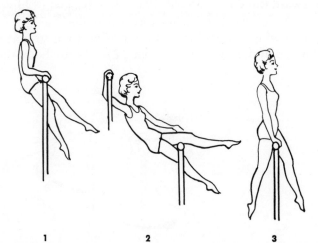

1   2   3

Fig. 6–15. Partial circle backward and extend legs to a crotch support on low bar.

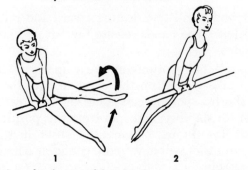

Fig. 6–16.   Swing the forward leg backward over the bar to a front support.

is placed under the thigh and one under the back to support her, if necessary, and guide her into the crotch support position.

TEACHING TECHNIQUES.   This stunt should be practiced a few times on the low bar before trying it from the high bar.

5. Swing the Forward Leg Backward over the Bar to a Front Support (Fig. 6–16).   If the left leg is forward and the right leg on the back side of the bar, the weight should be shifted to the right arm.   As the left leg is swung backward over the bar, the left hand reaches over the leg and grasps the bar again between the legs (1).   The weight is centralized on both hands in the front support position (2).

SPOTTING.   The spotter stands on the right side of the performer and helps her maintain balance by grasping her right arm.

6. Backward Hip Circle (Fig. 6–17).   In a backward hip circle the first step is to let the legs swing forward under the bar (1).   The legs are then whipped backward from this position so that the body moves upward and away from the bar (2).   As the body drops back

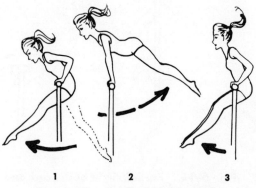

Fig. 6–17.   Backward hip circle.

Photo by Jim Fraser

Joyce Tanac Casting Backward in Preparation for a Backward Hip Circle on the Uneven Parallel Bars.

toward the bar, the arms are bent slightly so that the bar makes contact with the lower abdomen. The body is piked as it contacts the bar and the legs continue their forward motion under the bar (3). As the legs start upward to circle the bar, the upper body

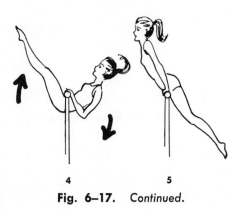

4   5

Fig. 6–17. *Continued.*

leans backward (4). The abdomen should maintain contact with the bar until the circle is completed in a front support position (5).

SPOTTING.   At least two spotters should be used.   The first spotter stands on the back side of the bar to one side of the performer and aids her in getting a good cast upward and away from the bar by lifting under the thigh with one hand and the abdomen with the other.   During this first part of the circle this spotter can also keep the performer in close to the bar.   The second spotter stands on the other side of the bar and, as the performer's legs come under the bar, places one hand under her thigh and one under her lower back to help her complete the circle.   Good spotters do not do all the work for the performer but only assist as required.

7. Squat Dismount to a Stand with the Back Toward the Bars (Fig. 6–18).   This stunt starts in the same manner as the backward hip circle.   The legs swing forward under the bar (1).   Next they are whipped backward and upward to a free front support, as in a backward hip circle, but the weight is shifted further forward over the bar and the hips are raised slightly (2).   The knees are pulled upward toward the chest, the body assuming a tuck position, so that the legs can pass over the bar between the arms (3).   As they pass over the bar, both hands thrust off the bar.   The body straightens as the feet clear the bar (4) and the performer drops to a stand with the back to the bars (5).

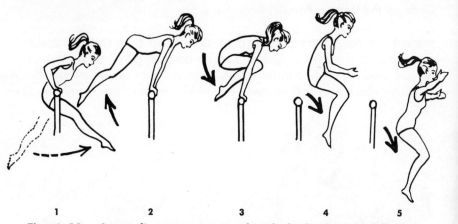

| 1 | 2 | 3 | 4 | 5 |

Fig. 6–18.   Squat dismount to a stand with the back toward the bars.

SPOTTING.   Two spotters are used.   One stands on the back side of the bar to the side of the performer and helps her get a good cast upward and away from the bar and, as the squat over the bar is started, helps her over the bar by lifting under her thigh.   This spotter should be very careful not to get her hands or arms caught between the performer and the bar. The second spotter stands on the dismount side of the bar and grasps the performer's upper arm. She helps the performer get the right amount of forward lean during the first part of the stunt, and as the bar is released she pulls the performer forward and helps her maintain balance on the landing. For extra safety four spotters, two on each side of the bar, may be used for this stunt.

TEACHING TECHNIQUES. The bar should be lowered as low as possible while this stunt is learned.

III. INTERMEDIATE ROUTINE IN DETAIL

1. Single Leg Swing-Up to Crotch Support (Fig. 6–19). The performer stands facing both the low and high bar and grasps the low bar in a regular grip (1). She jumps slightly off the floor and squats the left leg between the arms (2), hooks the leg over the bar, and swings forward in this position with the weight distributed equally between the arms and the back of the knee (3). As the back swing starts, the free leg is swung forcefully downward. The arms also press downward (4) and the body swings upward to a crotch support (5). The arms and free leg should remain straight throughout the whole stunt.

SPOTTING. The spotter stands on the same side of the bar and to one side of the performer and reaches under the bar with one hand to

1 2 3 4 5

Fig. 6–19. Single swing-up to crotch support.

grasp her free leg. This hand is used to pull down slightly on the free leg during the swing-up and to prevent the performer from going too far over the bar and falling forward as the stunt is completed. The other hand is placed under the small of the performer's back or under the buttocks to push her up into the crotch support.

TEACHING TECHNIQUE. Beginners should swing back and forth in the single knee hang under the bar and practice the single knee swing-up in this way.

2. Backward Crotch Circle (Fig. 6–20). After the mount the performer is in a crotch support on the low bar facing the high bar

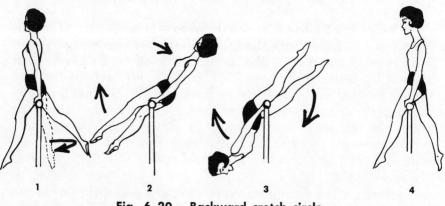

Fig. 6–20. Backward crotch circle.

with the left leg forward, the right leg back, and both hands in a regular grip. From this position the right leg is swung away from the bar (1). As it swings back to contact the bar again, the bar is gripped between the upper thighs and the upper body is leaned backward (2, 3). The performer should stretch away from the bar as far as possible during the backward and downward part of the circle and pull in toward the bar during the upward part. The stunt is completed in the crotch support position (4).

SPOTTING. A spotter is used on each side of the performer. They stand in front of the bar and reach underneath with the near hand to grasp the performer's wrist in a regular grip. During the last portion of the circle the other hand is used to lift under the performer's chest or shoulder to help her return to the crotch support.

3. Swing Right Leg from Crotch Support to Inner Seat. The weight is shifted to the left arm, and the right leg is swung up and over the low bar so that the performer finishes in a sitting position on the low bar facing the high bar. During this leg motion the right hand releases the low bar and shifts to a regular grip on the high bar.

Spotting. The spotter stands on the left side of the performer and supports her left arm to help her maintain balance as the leg and hand are shifted.

4. Drop to Hang on High Bar and Turn Half Right to Face Low Bar. There are a number of ways this half turn can be made. One method was described in Routine I. If the performer wishes to use another method, she certainly may do so.

5. Straddle Legs up and over Low Bar, Bounce Thighs off the Bar, and Pull to a Hip Swing-Up on High Bar (Fig. 6–21). The starting position is a hang on the high bar with a regular grip facing the low bar. The first movement is to raise the legs forward and at the same time straddle them wide apart (1). They should be raised well above the low bar and then placed together (2). From this position they are dropped hard onto the low bar making contact just above the back of the knee (3). A great deal of spring or rebound can be obtained in this way to start the hip-swing-up, or "pull-over" as it is

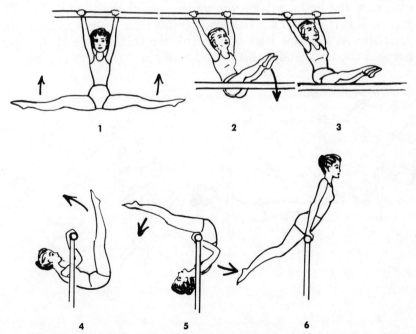

Fig. 6–21. Straddle legs up and over the low bar, bounce thighs off the bar, and pull to a hip swing-up on high bar.

commonly called. The legs are raised toward the upper bar by using the arm, chest, and abdominal muscles (4). The legs are actually pulled over the bar with the body in a pike position so that the lower abdomen makes contact with the bar (5). From this position the weight of the legs on one side of the bar should be enough to raise the upper body to the front support (6).

SPOTTING. The spotter stands underneath the high bar beside the performer. One hand is placed under the thighs to help the performer raise the legs in the straddle position. After the rebound off the low bar the spotter pushes under the lower back with one hand and on the top of the shoulder with the other hand, being sure to assist only as much as is necessary.

TEACHING TECHNIQUE. The pull-over should be learned first on the low bar. It can be started from a jump off the ground with one leg preceding the other. Spotters can assist much more readily when the stunt is done from the floor.

6. Roll Forward and Bounce off Back of Legs on Low Bar with One-Half Turn to Crotch Position (Fig. 6–22). From the support position on the high bar the motion of the hip swing-up is reversed. The head and upper body are tucked forward under the bar so that the weight of the body rests on the upper part of the thighs (1). The grip is shifted around the bar ready to take the weight in a hanging position. As the hips start downward, the thighs slide off the high bar and the hands take all the body weight. The legs are lowered

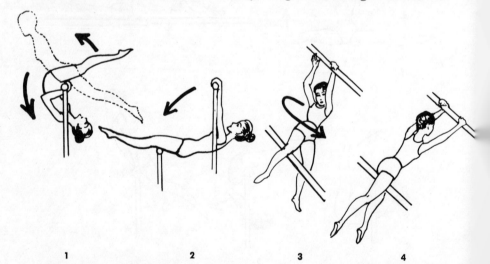

1   2   3   4

Fig. 6–22. Roll forward and bounce off back of legs on low bar with one-half turn to a crotch position.

forcefully during the latter part of the roll forward and are bounced off the back of the thighs on the low bar (2). As the legs rebound off the bar, the lower body is twisted to the left and the legs are spread (3) so that the left leg drops between the two bars and the right leg on the outside of the low bar. The left hand is not removed from the high bar, but the right hand has to be released and shifted to the other side of the left hand so that the half turn of the upper body can be completed. Upon completion of this stunt the performer is in a crotch seat on the low bar facing the high bar with the left hand in a reverse grip and the right hand in a regular grip on the high bar (4).

SPOTTING. The spotter stands between the bars slightly to the right of the performer. The hands are placed on the performer's hips as she lowers down for the rebound off the low bar. After the rebound the performer can be helped in the twisting motion by the spotter.

7. Swing Right Leg over the Bar to an Inner Seat. This movement has been described previously in this routine and also in Routine I. Although the hand positions are slightly different, it is not necessary to repeat the description. As the back leg is swung over the low bar, the left hand should be changed from a reverse to a regular grip on the high bar ready for the next stunt.

8. Lower to Hang on High Bar. If the performer leans forward and straightens the hips, the legs will slide off the low bar to the hanging position on the high bar.

9. Skin-the-Cat, Roll-Turn to One-Leg Squat on Low Bar (Fig. 6–23). From the hanging position on the high bar with the back to the low bar (1) the legs are tucked and raised up between the arms (2).

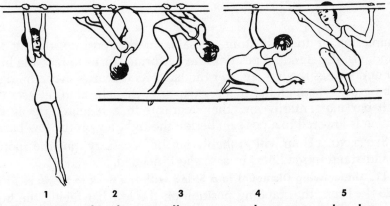

1   2   3   4   5

Fig. 6–23. Skin-the-cat, roll-turn to one-leg squat on low bar.

They are lowered as for a regular skin-the-cat position but, instead of lowering them all the way down, the fronts of the ankles are placed on the low bar (3). The right arm is released and the performer turns to the left under and around the left arm (4) and comes to a one-leg squat position on the right leg with the left leg stretched forward (5). The right hand grasps the low bar just below the right hip.

SPOTTING. The spotter stands between the bars and guides the performer's ankles into position during the first part of the stunt. Next the spotter supports the performer by the hips to make sure she doesn't lose her grip as the bar is released with the right hand. The spotter can also help the performer position herself during the last part of the movement.

10. Stand and Swing the Left Leg over the High Bar and back to the Low Bar (Fig. 6–24). This is a very simple stunt, but it adds beauty to the routine. The performer straightens the right leg and stands up on the low bar. The left leg, which was extended forward at the

Fig. 6–24. Stand and swing the left leg over the high bar and back to the low bar.

completion of the last stunt, remains in this position during the stand. In the standing position the performer turns to face the high bar and swings the left leg over the bar. As it swings over, the right hand grasps the high bar in a regular grip, the left hand releases the high bar momentarily and then regrasps in a regular grip as the left leg is lowered to a position beside the right leg on the low bar.

SPOTTING. Help will probably not be necessary, but the spotter should stand in readiness in case she is needed.

11. Underswing Dismount to a Stand with the Back to the Bars (Fig. 6–25). From the standing position on the low bar facing the high bar with the hands in a regular grip on the high bar the performer

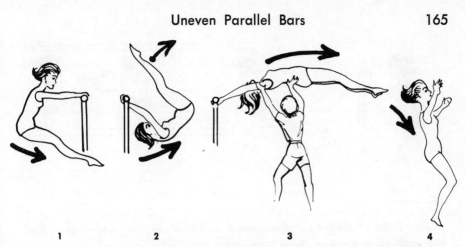

Fig. 6–25. Underswing dismount to a stand with the back to the bars.

jumps in the air and raises the legs forward in a pike position (1). The ankles are raised to the high bar as the forward swing develops (2). At the end of the forward swing the body is extended rapidly and the legs are shot upward and away from the bar. As the arched position is reached, the hands thrust off the bar (3) and the performer drops to a standing position on the mat facing away from the bars (4).

SPOTTING. The spotter stands underneath the high bar to the side of the performer. As the dismount is executed, one hand is placed on her shoulder and the other on the small of her back. As the performer approaches the ground, one hand is shifted across her chest and one hand across her back to assure she lands in balance. Because of the height of the high bar, a tall spotter should be used. The spotter cannot remain in a stationary position but must be quick to move in the direction of the dismount.

TEACHING TECHNIQUE. For safety this stunt must be taught on the low bar. The performer jumps off the floor and executes the stunt in the same way as described above. This makes spotting much easier and enables the spotter to practice spotting techniques while the performer is relatively safe at a low height.

IV. LOW ADVANCED ROUTINE IN DETAIL

1. Jump to a One-Legged Squat Stand on Low Bar and Grasp High Bar with an Immediate Half Turn (Fig. 6–26). This mount starts with a run of about fifteen feet and a takeoff from a beat board as in vaulting over the horse. The hands are placed on top of the low bar

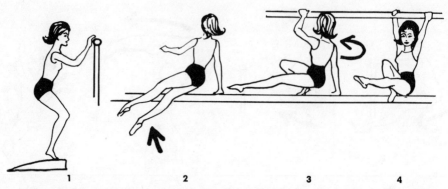

Fig. 6–26. Jump to a one-legged stand on low bar and grasp high bar with an immediate half turn.

in a regular grasp (1). Both hands press down hard as the hips are lifted up to the left (2). As the hips approach the top of the bar, the left hand releases the bar and grasps the high bar in a regular grip and the right leg bends so that the foot can be placed on the low bar (3). The right hand then releases the low bar and the performer pivots a half turn to the left with the weight partly resting on the right foot and partly being suspended from the left hand (4). The right hand grasps the high bar in a regular grip during the half turn. After the half turn the left hand, which was in a regular grip, will be in a reverse grip.

SPOTTING. Two spotters should be used. Both stand on the right side of the performer, one on the near side and one on the far side of the low bar. The near side spotter supports the right arm of the performer with one hand and lifts under her hips with the other hand during the first part of the mount. The far side spotter also grasps the performer's right arm during the first part of the mount, but as the right hand is released for the pivot she supports the performer's hips with both hands and follows her around during the turn.

TEACHING TECHNIQUE. A good lead-up stunt is a flank vault over the bar to a standing position on the mat or to a sitting position on the low bar. This mount can be learned more easily if both bars are lowered a little.

2. Kick Rise to Front Support on High Bar. As this stunt has been described in Routine II, it will not be redescribed in this routine. The left hand, which ends in a reverse grip after the first stunt of the routine, has to be quickly shifted to a regular grip before the kick rise is executed.

3. Forward Hip Circle (Fig. 6–27). The forward hip circle starts from the front support with a regular grip. Usually a reverse grip is used for a "forward" circle and a regular grip for a "backward" circle but the forward hip circle is an exception to this rule. The first step is to stretch as tall as possible in the front support position and to fall forward with the body straight (1). As the torso drops below the horizontal position, the head and upper body tuck rapidly under the bar. The arms bend and the hands shift their grip under the bar and then rapidly up on top of the bar (2). As the circle is completed, the upper body leans forward over the bar with the weight resting on the abdomen (3). The arms remain bent in this position.

Fig. 6–27.   Forward hip circle.

SPOTTING.   Use two spotters, one on each side of the bar and on both sides of the performer. The spotter at the back of the bar reaches under the bar with the near hand and grasps the performer's wrist with a regular grip. The other hand is used to lift under the performers back as the circle is completed. The spotter at the front of the bar helps the performer initiate the fast tucking movement of the upper body by pushing on the upper back with one hand, and delays the circling motion of the legs by holding the back of the thighs in close to the bar with the other hand.

TEACHING TECHNIQUE.   This stunt should be taught on the low bar where the spotters can readily reach the performer and where she is relatively safe.

4. Cast Back to Hang and Swing to Hip Circle on Low Bar (Fig. 6–28). If the forward hip circle is executed correctly, the legs will swing upward and backward as the circle is completed. This leg

1   2   3

Fig. 6–28. Cast back to hang and swing to hip circle on low bar.

movement helps lift the body away from the bar (1). At this time the performer pushes upward and away from the bar, then straightens the arms and swings downward and forward in a hanging position (2). The hips lead during the downward swing with the body in an arched position. As soon as the hips contact the low bar, the body is piked and wrapped around the bar and the high bar is released (3, 4). It is most important that the student does not pike before contacting the low bar, as this will result in a hard contact. The low bar is grasped in a regular grip and the backward hip circle is continued to the front support position (5).

SPOTTING. The spotter stands under the high bar and as the performer swings underneath places one hand under the upper back and one under the thighs and guides her into the hip circle.

TEACHING TECHNIQUES. The cast back should be practiced first without the hip circle. It can be practiced on the low bar dropping to a stand on the mat and then on the high bar with the spotter grasping the hips, with one hand in front and one behind, to control the swing and to catch the performer if she loses her grip. The hip circle should be mastered alone and then practiced from a swing back and forth under the high bar before it is tried from the cast back. Two spotters should swing the performer back and forth in the hang and spot carefully as the hip circle is attempted.

5. Squat-Through with Left Leg to Crotch Support (Fig. 6–29). This stunt is started by swinging both legs forward under the bar and then backward and upward. The body leans forward slightly with the arms straight and the hips raise backward and upward. The left leg is bent and the knee drawn up to the chest so that the foot can pass over the bar between the arms. The left leg is straightened and the hips lowered to a crotch support.

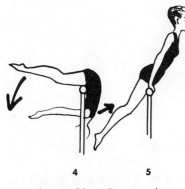

Fig. 6–28. *Continued.*

Photo by Jim Fraser

Dale McClements, 1962 National All-Round Champion, Casting Backward to a Hang on the High Bar in Preparation for a Forward Swing to a Backward Hip Circle on the Low Bar. It is not recommended that the average gymnast cast as high as Miss McClements as tremendous speed is attained by the time the gymnast contacts the low bar after casting as high as this.

Fig. 6–29. Squat through with left leg to crotch support.

SPOTTING.   The spotter stands in front of the bar and grasps the performer's upper arm or shoulder to help her maintain balance. Another spotter may be used, if necessary, at the back of the bar to help the performer raise the hips and squat the leg through.

6. Crotch Circle Forward with Regrasp of High Bar (Fig. 6–30). This is very similar to the knee circle forward described in Routine I and, except for the direction, the same as the crotch circle backward described in Routine III. The hands must be changed after the previous stunt to a reverse grip. To start the crotch circle the

1   2

Fig. 6–30. Crotch circle forward with regrasp of high bar.

performer lifts the legs up and off the bar; leans forward; stretches the head, trunk, and arms away from the bar; and squeezes the bar between the thighs (1). After half of the circle has been completed, the arms are used to pull the crotch tightly against the bar. As the performer approaches the verticle, she looks for the high bar, releases the low bar, and grasps the high bar in a regular grip (2).

SPOTTING. Two spotters stand on the back side of the bar one on each side of the performer. They reach under the bar with their near hands and grasp the performer's wrists in regular grips. As the performer completes the circle, their other hands support under the upper back at the time of the release of the low bar and grasp of the high bar.

7. Swing Right Leg Over to Sitting Position. This is a very simple movement that does not need to be described.

8. Arch Up to Stand with One-Half Turn to Face the High Bar (Fig. 6–31). The feet are placed on the low bar (1) and the weight is shifted forward over the feet. The hips and chest are raised to an arched stand on the low bar (2). The performer then turns slowly, shifting the hands and feet, as necessary, to a stand on the low bar facing the high bar (3).

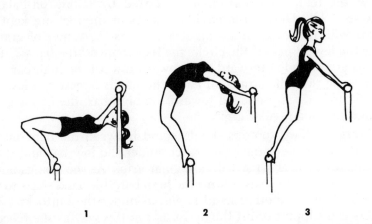

1   2   3

Fig. 6–31.   Arch up to stand with one-half turn to face the high bar.

SPOTTING. The spotter stands between the bars and pushes under the small of the performer's back to help her reach the arched position. She also stands in readiness as the performer turns from the arched to the standing position.

TEACHING TECHNIQUES. This stunt should be practiced with the feet on the floor and the hands on the low bar. Considerable limbering work will also have to be done on the mats to prepare the performer for the arched position.

9. Backward Sole Circle on Low Bar with Cast to Regrasp High Bar (Fig. 6–32). The performer releases the high bar and bends forward to grasp the low bar in a regular grip with one hand on each

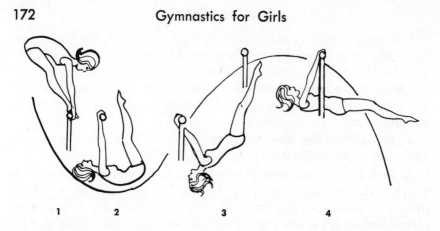

Fig. 6–32.   Backward sole circle on low bar with cast to regrasp high bar.

side of the feet. The sole circle is started by falling off-balance backward (1). During the circle the soles of the feet are kept on the bar with the knees and arms straight. As the center of gravity passes the lowest part of the circle, the feet come off the bar (2) and the legs are extended forward and upward toward the high bar (3). At the same time the arms pull hard, the hands release the low bar and, as the body is propelled toward the high bar, the hands grasp the high bar in a regular grip (4).

SPOTTING. Two spotters should stand between the bars one on each side of the performer and reach under the low bar and grasp the performer's near wrist with a regular grip. As she swings under the bar and starts the cast toward the high bar, this hand shifts to the upper back and the other hand is placed under the buttocks. The spotters can support or lift the performer in this way as she releases the low bar and regrasps the high bar.

10. Skin-the-Cat, Roll-Turn to Squat on Low Bar. Following the previous stunt there will be a downward and backward swing that might result in the performer hitting the low bar with the buttocks. On the forward swing following this the legs are raised to execute a skin-the-cat and roll turn in the same manner as described in Routine III except that the left hand releases the bar in this routine.

11. Kick-Up to Momentary Handstand with One Hand on Low Bar, One Hand on High Bar, and Then Immediately Fall over High Bar to Front Support (Fig. 6–33). After the roll-turn to squat position on the low bar (1), the left hand is placed in front of the left foot in a regular grip on the low bar. The left leg is straightened so that the hips are raised (2). From this position the right leg is raised back-

1   2   3

4   5   6

Fig. 6–33. Kick-up to momentary handstand with one hand on low bar, one hand on high bar, and then immediately fall over high bar to front support.

ward in the air. The left leg kicks off the low bar (3) and both legs are joined in a momentary handstand position (4), following which the abdomen is leaned against the high bar and the legs are dropped over the bar in a pike position (5). The left arm is then transfered to the high bar and the upper body is raised to the front support position (6).

SPOTTING. The spotter stands on the low bar in front of the performer and leans against the high bar for stability. As the performer kicks up to the handstand, she catches the performer's hips or the back of her thighs (she will be facing the back of the performer in the handstand position). She can also guide the performer during the fall across the high bar to the front support. As the performer becomes more proficient, the spotter should stand on the floor between the bars and place one hand on the performers shoulder and one hand on her upper back to prevent her from overbalancing.

12. Handstand on Low Bar, One-Quarter Turn Dismount to a Stand on the Mat (Fig. 6–34).   From the front support on the high bar the performer leans forward and grasps the low bar with the left hand in a reverse grip and the right hand in a regular grip (1).   From this position the legs are lowered slightly and then whipped up into the air to a handstand on the low bar (2).   The body is turned immediately to the left and the right hand pushes hard off the bar (3). The performer drops to the mat to a stand with the left hand still on the low bar (4).

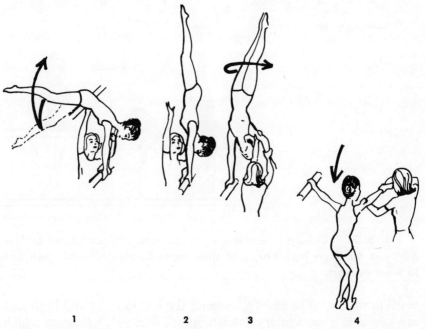

Fig. 6–34.   Handstand on low bar, one-quarter turn dismount to a stand on the mat.

SPOTTING.   Use two spotters, one on each side of the low bar. The spotter between the bars grasps the performer's left upper arm with one hand and pushes on her hip with the other hand to make sure she clears the bar. The spotter on the dismount side stands in front of the performer and grasps her right upper arm. As the performer pushes off with this arm, the spotter steps back, pulls her away from the bar, and then helps her maintain balance on the landing.

Teaching Techniques. Drape a mat over the low bar so that the performer will land on a padded surface if she fails to clear the bar on the dismount.

V. ADVANCED ROUTINE IN DETAIL

1. Glide-Kip (Fig. 6–35). This mount starts in a standing position under the high bar with both hands in a regular grip on the low bar. The performer jumps upward and raises the hips backward so that the body is in a pike position (1). As the swing starts forward, the feet glide a few inches from the floor until a fully extended position is reached (2). At this point the body pikes rapidly and the ankles are raised up to the bar. The backward swing is completed in this inverted pike position (3). At the end of the backward swing there is a rapid extension of the body which raises the hips close to the bar (4). The legs are thrust upward and outward during this body extension so that the bar slides up the front of the legs from the ankles to the hips. Some teachers say this motion can be likened to pulling a pair of sweat pants up from the ankles to the waist. After this kipping motion, the legs swing downward and backward, the upper body swings upward and forward, and the hands press down hard and then shift up on top of the bar. The performer ends in a front support position (5).

Spotting. The spotters stand at the back of the bar on each side of the performer and place one hand under the back of the thigh as soon as it can be reached and one hand under the upper back. The performer can be manipulated through most of the stunt by two good spotters.

1   2   3   4   5

Fig. 6–35. Glide-kip.

Photo by Jim Fraser

Joyce Tanac Executing a Glide-Kip on the Uneven Parallel Bars.

TEACHING TECHNIQUES. A girl who can do a good snap-up on the tumbling mats will learn the kip faster than a girl who cannot. The snap-up might be called the first stunt in the kip progression. Next the performer should practice the kip on a low horizontal bar about chest height (or on a lowered parallel bar) by jumping immediately into the pike position with the ankles close to the bar. By eliminating the glide the performer can concentrate on the kipping motion and practice only the second part of the glide-kip. The next step is to practice walkout glide kips. Instead of gliding the feet forward the feet run forward in short fast steps on the ground to the extended position. Spotters are very important in this learning process on a low bar. One extra spotter can be used on the front side of the bar to help the performer reach the fully extended position and then help her get her ankles up to the bar.

2. Backward Hip Circle. This stunt has been described in Routine II.

3. Squat Feet Up to Stand on Low Bar (Fig. 6–36). This starts in the same way as the squat dismount in Routine II. From the support position the legs are swung forward under the bar (1). They are then cast upward and backward away from the bar. The hips are raised slightly during this cast (2). As the height of the cast is reached, the knees are raised to the chest and the feet are placed on the bar (3). As the feet are placed on the bar, the performer turns slightly to the left, looks quickly over the left shoulder for the high bar, and places the left hand on top of the bar (4). She then stands up, turns, and faces away from the high bar again, reaches backward with the right hand, and places it on top of the high bar (5). The hands should be two or three times shoulder width apart.

| 1 | 2 | 3 | 4 | 5 |

Fig. 6–36.   Squat feet up to stand on low bar.

SPOTTING. The spotter stands facing the performer with the low bar between them and helps the performer maintain balance during the squat up by supporting her right arm.

4. Shoot to Dislocate and Swing to Hip Circle (Fig. 6–37). From the standing position on the low bar with the hands quite wide apart on the high bar the performer bends forward from the waist and raises the hips slightly (1). The next step is to spring off the low bar so that the hips pass between the arms into an "inverted pike hang" on the high bar (2). In this position the performer will swing backward under the high bar (3). Toward the end of this backward swing the legs are thrust upward and backward, the body is extended

1   2   3   4

Fig. 6–37.   Shoot to dislocate and swing to hip circle.

to an arch, and the shoulders are "dislocated." The performer swings downward and forward in a slightly arched position (4, 5). The hip circle is executed exactly as described in Routine IV (6, 7).

SPOTTING. Spotting during the learning process is explained under teaching techniques. Once the stunt has been learned well enough to include it in a routine the spotter should stand in readiness under the high bar during the extension and move quickly between the bars to spot the hip circle.

TEACHING TECHNIQUES. Both the jump into position and the shoot to dislocate can be learned on the low bar. The jump into the inverted pike hang is practiced by jumping off a bench into the hang on the low bar. One spotter assists by lifting under the abdomen to help the performer lift her hips between her arms while another spotter on the other side of the performer supports under the back in case the performer looses her grip. The progression in learning the dislocate is as follows:

a. Do a skin-the-cat on the low bar, place the feet on the mat, and "dislocate" the shoulders. It may be necessary to lower the bar. The learner can work up gradually to the dislocate from a swing in the inverted pike-hang. The bar should be low enough, however, to permit the feet to land on the ground before the arms have to support the weight.
b. Shoot for a dislocate on the low bar but have two spotters take all the weight of the body by lifting under the hips at the time the shoulders are "dislocated."
c. Try the same thing on the high bar and have two spotters reach up and take the weight by supporting under the hips.

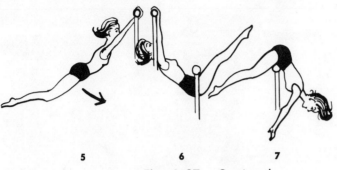

5   6   7

Fig. 6–37. *Continued.*

5. Eagle from Low Bar to High Bar (Fig. 6–38). The term "eagle" is used so often in both men's and women's gymnastics that this common name will be used rather than trying to describe this stunt with other terminology. As the hip circle is completed, the body is extended rapidly from the pike position with the stomach resting on the bar (1). This movement, together with the spring from the bar, will propel the performer away from the bar in a backward direction. The arms are spread about two or two and one-half shoulder widths apart and grasp the high bar in a "rotated" reverse grip (2). (When the performer is hanging from the bar with a reverse grip the palms of the hands face the opposite direction from the performer.

1   2

Fig. 6–38. Eagle from low bar to high bar.

Photo by Jim Fraser

Dale McClements executing an eagle on the uneven parallel bars.
Note the rotated position of the hands used in the grasp for the eagle.
In this picture Dale has just left the low bar and is in the air prior to
grasping the high bar. The angle of the picture is somewhat mislead-
ing, as it appears her arms will hit the high bar, but actually the bar
will be grasped in the hands.

In a rotated reverse grip the hands are turned 360 degrees, the left
hand counter clockwise, the right hand clockwise, so that the palms
of the hands are still facing the opposite direction from the performer.)

SPOTTING. As the performer leaves the bar after the hip circle,
the spotter places one hand on the abdomen and one hand on the
back and assists her in regrasping the high bar. The spotter should
also be alert to prevent the performer from overturning and landing
on her back if the bar is missed.

TEACHING TECHNIQUES (Fig. 6–39). Two spotters stand between
the bars one on each side of the performer. The performer stands
on the spotters thighs and leans across and rests her weight on the
low bar in a pike position. The performer then extends rapidly and

Fig. 6–39.   Teaching techniques for eagle.

completes the eagle while still standing on the spotters' thighs. The spotters assist by first stabilizing and then lifting the performer's thighs if necessary.

6. Stand on Low Bar (Fig. 6–40). After completing the eagle, the feet are placed on the low bar (1) and the legs straightened to a standing position (2). The hands do not release or move on the high bar, but push away and press down to assist in reaching the standing position.

1   2

Fig. 6–40.   Stand on low bar.

7. Straddle Jump Backward over High Bar with Regrasp and Swing to a Hip Circle on Low Bar (Fig. 6–41). From the standing position on the low bar both hands are lowered to the side and the body is leaned slightly backward (1). As the weight shifts backward, the performer jumps upward and backward over the bar. The hips lead in a pike position with the legs straddled wide apart. As soon as

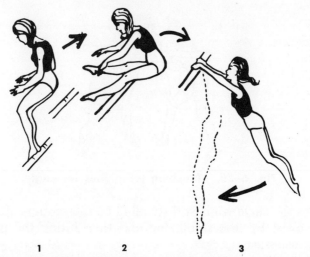

1   **2**   **3**

Fig. 6–41. Straddle jump backward over high bar with regrasp and swing to a hip circle on low bar.

the crotch passes over the high bar, the hands grasp the bar between the legs in a regular grip (2). As the feet pass over the bar, they are closed together and extended backward so that the performer is in a hanging position on the high bar (3). In this position she swings forward and executes the hip circle in the same manner as described in Routine IV.

SPOTTING. Explained with teaching techniques.

TEACHING TECHNIQUES. This stunt should be practiced over the low bar with the high bar removed. If possible the low bar should be set slightly lower than regulation height. The performer stands on a bench or table, jumps over the low bar, and lands standing on the floor. The regrasp can be practiced at this time, but the arms are not required to assume any weight. The spotter stands behind the performer and grasps her hips as she jumps over the bar to support her if she catches her feet and falls backward. When the stunt is first done from the low bar over the high bar, it is advisable to use an overhead safety belt. If one is not available, two excellent spotters should be placed behind the performer to catch her if necessary. This stunt can be learned in easy stages by jumping to a straddle sitting position on the high bar and grasping the bar between the legs while the legs are in contact with the bar.

8. Cast with a Half Turn Backward to a Squat Stand on the Low Bar (Fig. 6–42). As the hip circle is completed, the legs swing forward under the low bar (1). From this position they reverse direction

and swing backward and upward until the body is clear of the bar
and the weight is supported on the hands (2). At this time the hips
are raised, the knees are drawn up to the chest in a tuck position and
one hand pushes away from the low bar initiating a backward turn
(3). The hand that thrusts off the low bar is shifted quickly to
grasp the high bar in a regular grip and the feet are placed on the
low bar to the outside of the other hand. The half turn has now
been completed and the performer is in a squat position on the low
bar with one hand on the low bar and one hand on the high bar (4).

1   2   3   4

**Fig. 6–42.   Cast with a half turn backward to a squat stand on the
low bar.**

SPOTTING. The spotter stands on the outside of the low bar
almost in front of the hand that will remain on the bar. She grasps
the performer's upper arm and helps her maintain her balance during
the movement. The spotter must stay out of the way of the legs, as
they swing under the low bar at the start of the stunt, and then shift
position so as to be out of the way as the feet are placed on the bar.

**9. Backward Sole Circle and Cast to Hang on High Bar with One-
Half Turn** (Fig. 6–43). This stunt is almost identical to the backward sole circle with cast that was described in Routine IV. To
get into position to start the sole circle the hand from the high bar
has to be shifted to the low bar and the hand on the low bar has to
be changed to a regular grip. The legs are straightened and the sole
circle and cast are then executed in exactly the same manner as
previously described up to the point of regrasp on the high bar.
As the performer reaches for the high bar, the hands are crossed (1).
The left hand grasps in a regular grip, the right reaches under the
wrist of the left arm and secures a reverse grip about six inches to
the left of the left hand. The performer starts to turn toward the

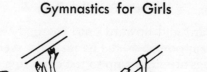

1　　　　　2　　　　　3

Fig. 6–43. Backward sole circle and cast to hang on the high bar with one-half turn.

right hand (this is actually a left turn) as soon as the right hand grasps the high bar (2). There is a natural swing backward toward the low bar after the grasp of the high bar. During this swing the turn is completed so that the performer will be facing the low bar by the time the stomach makes contact with it (3).

SPOTTING. The spotting is the same as described for the "sole circle cast to regrasp" in Routine IV, but in this case the spotters can also aid in the execution of the half turn.

1　　　　　2　　　　　3

Fig. 6–44. Stomach-whip on low bar, place feet on low bar, and kick-rise to front support on high bar.

10. Stomach-Whip on low bar, Place Feet on Low Bar, and Kick-Rise to Front Support on High Bar (Fig. 6–44).   After the completion of the previous stunt the performer is hanging on the high bar and swinging toward the low bar facing the bar. The abdomen makes contact with the bar and the legs continue forward and swing slightly under the bar in a pike position (1).   From this position the legs whip backward as the body starts to swing backward away from the bar (2).   On the next forward swing the left hand is shifted to a regular grip and the legs are raised (3) permitting the feet to be placed on the low bar with the knees bent (4).   The next part of this series is very similar to the single leg kick-rise described in Routine II and repeated in Routine IV except that in this case both legs kick off the low bar. The legs are straightened rapidly and push backward and upward away from the bar. The arms pull and press downward and the performer rises to the front support position on the high bar (5, 6).

Spotting.   The spotter stands underneath the high bar to the side of the performer ready to catch her if she loses her grip during the stomach-whip and assists in the kick-rise by pushing under her buttocks.

11. Squat-Through to Stand on Low Bar (Fig. 6–45). As there have been several lead-up skills included in previous routines for this stunt, it should not be difficult for a performer who has pro-

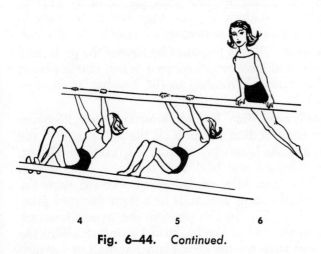

4   5   6

Fig. 6–44. *Continued.*

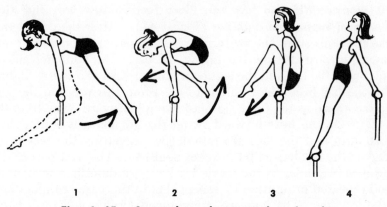

Fig. 6–45.   Squat-through to stand on low bar.

gressed satisfactorily this far. The squat dismount in Routine II, the single leg squat through in Routine IV, and the squat up to stand described earlier in this routine are all very similar. This stunt starts exactly the same as the squat dismount (1), but as the legs are brought through between the hands (2) the performer leans backward slightly and maintains the grip on the high bar (3). The weight is partially supported by the hands until the feet land on the low bar (4).

SPOTTING.   During the learning process two spotters stand on the low bar leaning against the high bar and assist the performer by grasping her upper arm as she squats over and lowers her feet to the low bar. When the performer first tries the stunt by herself, the spotters should stand underneath the high bar to be alert in case of a fall and also to guide the performer's feet onto the low bar.

TEACHING TECHNIQUES.   Teach the stunt by having the performer squat over the low bar and lower to stand on a bench that is placed in approximately the same relationship to the low bar as the low bar is to the high bar.

12. Jump Backward over High Bar to Straddle Cutoff Dismount (Fig. 6–46).   From the standing position on the low bar with the back to the high bar and the hands in a regular grip on the high bar, the performer jumps upward and backward to a rear support in a pike position (1). She then falls off balance backward with the hips dropping between the arms and ends in a tight inverted pike-hang underneath the bar (2). In this position she swings forward, then backward, and at the end of the backward swing straddles the legs, presses down and then releases the hands, and leans forward from the waist (3, 4). This is a straddle cutoff forward. As the legs are straddled, they stretch upward and sideward rather than immediately downward. The landing is in a stand facing the bars (5).

SPOTTING. Two spotters stand to the rear and slightly to the side of the performer as she jumps backward over the bar. They reach with both hands for the upper back and make contact as soon as possible and maintain contact until the release. They can help by pushing a little at the time the bar is released but should be careful not to push too hard as this might result in the performer landing on her face. The spotters' hold should be maintained until the landing to make sure that the performer lands in balance.

TEACHING TECHNIQUES. Teach the jump backward from a bench over the low bar. The straddle cutoff should also be practiced from the low bar where the spotters can more readily reach the performers.

1   2   3   4   5

Fig. 6–46. Jump backward over high bar to straddle cutoff dismount.

7

Trampoline

There are many different versions of the origin of the trampoline. The term has been used in the past to refer to many different types of circus acts. The dictionary defines "trampoline" as an exhibition on stilts. "Trampolin" in Spanish means "diving board." The idea for the modern trampoline probably came from aerial performers doing tumbling stunts in their safety net after dismounting from their trapeze.

Whatever the history may be, the modern trampoline, the piece of equipment as we know it today, has been developed in the United States in very recent years. Trampolining is the only gymnastic event that is truly American. The trampoline was first manufactured in quantity in 1937 by George Nissen of Cedar Rapids, Iowa, and until recently the term "trampoline" was the trade name for the Nissen Trampoline. The trampoline event was first officially introduced into men's collegiate competition in 1948 and into A.A.U. competition in 1954. Since the Second World War the activity has grown greatly in popularity throughout the United States and Canada. The equipment is now manufactured in Europe and Japan and is rapidly growing in popularity throughout the world. The trampoline is not a recognized international event, however, for either men or women and has never been an event in the Olympic games.

The trampoline has done a lot for the sport of gymnastics in our country. It appeals to younger children. Thousands of boys and girls have first become interested in the trampoline and later this interest has carried over to the other events.

At the time of writing there is another term being used for "trampolining." In the Amateur Athletic Union Rule Book it is known as "rebound tumbling." This term was also used in the collegiate rules for a period of two years. Teachers should be familiar with the term "rebound tumbling" as many written sources use this rather than "trampolining."

VALUES

Trampolining develops timing, coordination, a sense of balance, and control of the body in the air. The trampoline is also an excellent event for developing cardiovascular and respiratory fitness. It looks easy when you watch someone else bounce, but actually it takes considerable energy and good conditioning to bounce continuously for a period of just a couple of minutes. Trampolining is primarily a lower body activity. More can be accomplished in this event, than in the other five events, by the girl who lacks upper body strength, or by the girl who is overweight and can't handle her weight in the other events.

The trampoline can be used as a training aid for other gymnastic events. Many tumbling stunts, floor exercise movements, and dismounts from the beam and uneven parallel bars can be taught first on the trampoline. The trampoline can also be used in teaching diving or as a conditioning activity for skiers or other athletes. Probably one of the greatest values of trampolining is the indirect value resulting from the enjoyment of the activity. It is fun to bounce. Students can relax, forget their worries, bounce their cares away, and thus improve their mental health.

SAFETY

Trampolining is somewhat dangerous, but so are many other physical education activities such as swimming and skiing. Automobiles are potentially far more dangerous than trampolines. With proper instruction and emphasis on safety procedures it can be made relatively safe. Most of the general safety procedures mentioned in Chapter 1 apply to the trampoline. Some of these should be re-emphasized when instruction in this event is given.

The following points are the most important:

1. Do not allow any horseplay, especially horseplay that involves more than one on the trampoline at a time. This does not mean that two people cannot bounce at once. Instruction should be given in double bouncing. However, this text does not include this phase of trampolining.

2. A performer should never work out alone. A spotter is essential for many stunts. The spotter should be on the end of the trampoline, either in front of, or behind the performer, depending on the stunt. It might be wise to require two spotters at all times—one at each end—so that the performer can execute stunts facing either direction. For extra safety a spotter might be placed on each side of the trampoline as well as on the ends, but spotters are seldom needed on the sides.

3. Encourage controlled bouncing. Excessively high bouncing should be forbidden.

4. Teach students how to get on and off (especially off) the trampoline. Do not let them bounce from the trampoline to the floor until they have reached the expert level. The hands should be placed on the frame of the trampoline when climbing off.

5. Do not allow inexperienced girls to use the trampoline unless supervised. Perhaps it should be kept locked and made available outside of class only to those who are well qualified.

6. Probably the most important safety precaution is to follow the right progression of stunts. Students should be taught to progress slowly, to overlearn fundamentals, and to try new stunts only when they are positive they are ready for them. They should progress especially slowly and spot carefully when the somersault stage is reached.

7. Teach the technique of stopping the bounce or "killing the bounce" by flexing the knees upon contact with the bed. A performer should learn to judge when the center of gravity is not over her feet on a landing and use this technique of "killing the bounce" to prevent flying off onto the floor.

8. Frame pads are a necessity. They should be inspected regularly to see that they are securely fastened and cover all the metal frame.

9. Give instruction in unfolding and folding the trampoline. Many students have been injured because teachers have failed to do this and the trampoline has unfolded on them as they are setting it up or putting it away.

TEACHING HINTS

There are several general teaching hints that will help to make trampoline instruction successful. Assign three, or at the most five, students to a trampoline. Students who are waiting their turn should spot and learn by watching others perform. Performers should be limited in time, or in number of bounces, or number of stunts tried, each time they get on the trampoline. When this "time limit," "bounce limit," or "stunt limit" is completed, they should quickly climb off. The next student in line should be ready to climb or roll on just as quickly.

Before teaching stunts on the trampoline a beginner must learn a controlled bounce. A performer bounces with the feet about shoulder width apart for lateral stability. The feet may be brought together in the air and the toes pointed, but this should not be stressed for the beginner as she has enough to think about without this. The toes contact the bed first, but the heels also make contact, and the knees bend slightly as the performer sinks into the bed. The knees straighten vigorously on the rebound from the bed. The arms go through a circular motion during the bounce. They lift up the front of the body and reach overhead on the upward flight and move downward laterally or out to the side of the body during the downward flight. This circular motion is made with the arms relaxed and slightly bent and should not be exaggerated. The eyes look at the frame on the end of the trampoline. A performer should try to do all her bouncing on or near the center cross on the bed and should always face the end, not the side, of the trampoline.

RULES

Trampoline rules are in the process of change at the time this book is being written. Women's rules call for two eight-bounce routines. Men's A.A.U. rules call for two ten-bounce routines. Men's collegiate rules have just been changed to one routine consisting of at least ten and not more than twelve contacts with the bed after the start of the first stunt. The authors are reasonably sure that this plan will also be adopted for women's rules in the near future. Therefore the routines in this chapter are composed of a single series of eleven contacts with the bed of the trampoline.

In competition the performer is allowed a reasonable number of preparatory bounces before the start of her routine. The count starts on the landing of the first stunt in the series. If more than twelve contacts are made after the start of the routine, any stunt or part of a stunt performed after the twelfth landing is discounted by the judges and a slight deduction of points made for lack of planning and control. An official counts the number of landings.

All exercises must begin and terminate on the bed of the trampoline. If a performer in the course of her performance touches anything save the bed of the trampoline, or is prevented by spotters from doing so, her routine terminates at that moment and she is scored on her performance up to that point.

It is wise for a performer to plan a routine of ten or eleven bounces rather than twelve bounces. On many occasions she will get off balance during her routine and be forced to take an extra bounce. If she has one bounce to spare she will be able to take this extra bounce and continue her routine as planned without going over the maximum of twelve bounces. In advanced work an extra back somersault is used, rather than an extra bounce, to enable the performer to regain balance before performing the next more difficult stunt in her routine.

In this chapter all routines have eleven contacts with the bed after the start of the first stunt. This allows for one extra bounce somewhere during the routine in case a girl loses control and needs to regain her balance before continuing. Extra bounces should not be taken unless absolutely necessary as they are considered a fault, or break in the routine, and are penalized severely by judges.

ABBREVIATED ROUTINE DESCRIPTIONS

   I. Stag leap to feet, knee drop, feet, seat drop, feet, half pirouette to feet, hands and knee drop, feet, front drop, feet, arch jump to feet.
  II. Half pirouette to front drop, feet, knee drop, seat drop, half twist to feet, full pirouette to feet, seat drop, half twist to seat drop, feet, back drop, feet.
 III. Half twist to back drop, half twist to feet, straddle touch toes to feet, front drop, half turntable to front drop, feet, back drop, front drop, feet, back drop, pull over to feet.
  IV. Full pirouette to seat drop, full twist to seat drop, feet, back drop, half twist to back drop (cradle), half twist to feet, tuck bounce to feet, back somersault, seat drop, feet, front somersault.
   V. Layout back somersault, baroni, back somersault, front one-and-one-quarter somersault, feet, split leap to feet, three quarter back somersault, feet, stag leap to feet, back one and a quarter somersault, pull over to feet.

Other more advanced stunts explained:
   1. Cody to feet,
   2. Full twisting back somersault,
   3. One and a half twisting front somersault,
   4. Double back somersault.

I. BEGINNING ROUTINE IN DETAIL

1. Stag Leap (Fig. 7–1).   The performer may take as many preliminary bounces as necessary, but the desired height can be
reached and control attained after three or four bounces when the
opening stunt in the routine is not difficult.   The opening stunt in
this routine is merely a posed leap in the air.   At the height of the
jump the girl stretches one leg straight out behind and raises the
other knee forward with the knee bent so that the lower leg points
back in the same direction as the straight leg.   The arms may as-

1   2

Fig. 7–1.   Stag leap.

sume a number of positions, there is no set rule as long as the position is graceful.   Usually both arms are kept almost straight, the
one on the bent leg side stretches above the head and the other
slightly above horizontal in the same direction as the straight leg (1).
This position is held momentarily and then the body returns to the
normal verticle position ready for the landing (2).

2. Knee Drop (Fig. 7–2).   As the performer bounces into the air
following the stag leap the lower legs are raised backward.   The
landing is made on the knees, shins, and insteps of the legs.   The
knees should be slightly apart for balance.   The back should be
straight or very slightly flexed (1).   If the back is arched on the
landing, there is a tendency for the hips to snap further forward.
This seldom results in injury, but it can be momentarily painful.
If the hips are flexed too much, there will be very little rebound.

Fig. 7–2. Knee drop.

1

The arms go through the same motions as during a regular bounce. This has already been explained in the introduction of this chapter. The head should be kept erect with the eyes focused on the frame at the end of the trampoline.

TEACHING TECHNIQUES.   The stunt should be learned with a very low bounce.

3. Seat Drop (Fig. 7–3).   Following the knee drop the performer returns to the feet (1).   This is the third contact with the bed after the start of the routine.   As the performer leaves the bed again, the body leans slightly backward and the legs are raised forward in a pike position (2).   The landing on the bed is with the legs straight forward, the trunk slightly behind vertical, the head erect, and the hands on the bed slightly behind the hips with the fingers pointing toward the toes (3).   As the performer rebounds from the trampoline, the hands give a push from the bed, the trunk is leaned forward, and the legs are pulled backward under the body.

TEACHING TECHNIQUES.   This stunt should be learned with very little bounce.

1   2   3

Fig. 7–3. Seat drop.

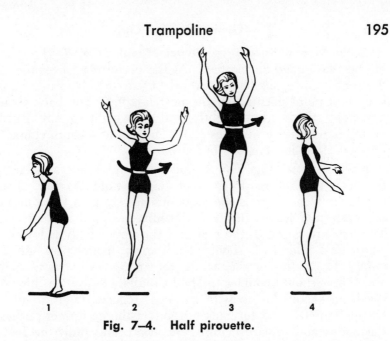

Fig. 7–4. Half pirouette.

4. Half Pirouette (Fig. 7–4). Following the seat drop the performer returns to the feet (1). This is the fourth contact with the bed. A pirouette is nothing more than a half turn in the air with the body vertical. As the performer leaves the bed for the next bounce, the head and upper body start to turn to the left (or right) (2). The arms lift in the normal way but continue to a position straight above the head so that they are a continuation of the longitudinal axis of the body as the height of the bounce is reached (3). The head should be erect. Looking down at the bed on a pirouette will usually result in landing off balance. When the half turn has been completed, the arms go out to the side to stop the twisting motion and to be ready for the next landing (4).

Fig. 7–5. Hands and knee drop.

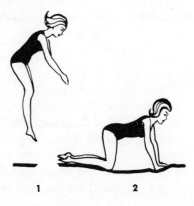

5. Hands and Knee Drop (Doggie Drop) (Fig. 7–5). The half pirouette is ended on the feet. As the performer leaves the bed on the next bounce, she leans forward (1) so as to land in a hand and knee four-point position on the next landing. The back should be horizontal, the head up slightly, and the weight equally distributed on the hands and lower legs (2). This is the seventh contact with the bed after the start of the routine.

6. Front Drop (Fig. 7–6). Following the hands and knee drop the performer returns to the feet (eighth contact) (1). The next stunt, the front drop, is the most difficult stunt in this routine. As the performer leaves the bed, the hips are used as a pivot point. The legs are raised to the rear and the upper body is lowered forward (2). The hips should land approximately on the takeoff point. The palms of the hands, forearms, lower chest, abdomen, and thighs should contact the bed simultaneously. In this position the head should be up with the eyes focused on the end of the trampoline (3). To get back to the feet the performer pushes with the hands and forearms, raises the head, and pulls the feet back under the hips as she rebounds from the bed (4).

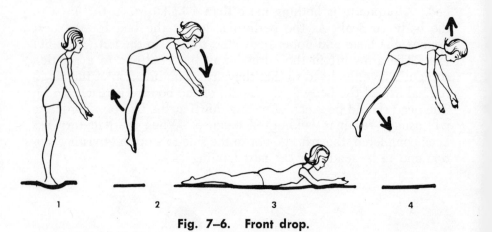

1   2   3   4

Fig. 7–6.   Front drop.

TEACHING TECHNIQUES. The first step is to lie flat on the bed and assume the prone position described above. The next step is to do the front drop immediately after a hand knee drop. The body and head are in the right position in the hand knee drop so the only movement involved is to straighten the legs and reach forward slightly with the arms and drop to the prone position. The next step is to stand on the bed with the knees slightly flexed and bend

1 2

Fig. 7–7. Arch jump.

forward at the waist so that the trunk is horizontal. From this position spring slightly with the legs, raise them backward, and land in the front drop. A common mistake on the front drop is to dive forward. In lead-ups it should be stressed that the hips drop straight down and land on the bed immediately under their starting position.

7. Arch Jump (Fig. 7–7). This is another pose in the air. After the front drop the performer returns to the feet (tenth contact). As she leaves the bed on the next rebound, the arms are stretched overhead, the head dropped backward, the back arched, and the knees flexed (1). A flexible girl can almost touch her heels to her head in this pose. To finish the routine the performer returns to the straight body vertical position for a controlled landing in balance with the feet remaining in contact with the bed and the arms raised to the side (2).

II. LOW INTERMEDIATE ROUTINE IN DETAIL

1. Half Pirouette to Front Drop (Fig. 7–8). This is a combination of two stunts in Routine I. It is a beautiful stunt if done high off the bed in an arched position all the way. As the performer leaves the bed she leans backward, looks over one shoulder, and starts to twist the upper body in the same direction (1). The hips are used as a pivot point with the legs being raised and the upper body lowered (2). The arms are usually kept out to the side like the wings of a bird during this stunt rather than being raised above

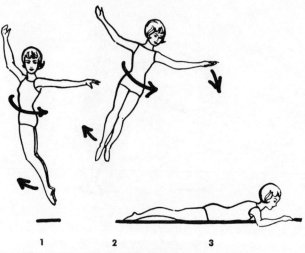

Fig. 7–8. Half pirouette to front drop.

the head as in the half pirouette. The landing on the bed is the same as for a regular stomach drop (3). The performer has now turned 180 degrees and is facing the opposite direction.

TEACHING TECHNIQUES. This stunt can be done to a hand and knee landing first.

2. Knee Drop. Following the front drop landing the performer returns to the feet (second bed contact). The next stunt is the knee drop, which has already been described in Routine I. This is the third contact with the bed.

3. Seat Drop Half Twist to Stand (Fig. 7–9). The seat drop has also been described in Routine I. In this routine, however, the seat drop immediately follows the knee drop without the feet touching the bed of the trampoline in between the two stunts. This is not a difficult move. It just involves raising the legs forward as the performer rebounds from the knee landing. The seat drop is the fourth contact with the bed in the routine (1). As the performer returns to the feet following the seat drop, a 180 degree turn is made so that she lands on the feet facing the opposite direction (fifth contact). This is the same movement as the half pirouette described in Routine I except that it starts from a seat drop instead of from the feet. As the performer rebounds from the bed, the arms lift above the head and the head and upper body start to twist to the right (or left) (2). The legs are pulled back under the body, but by the time they reach the vertical position the half twist has been completed (3).

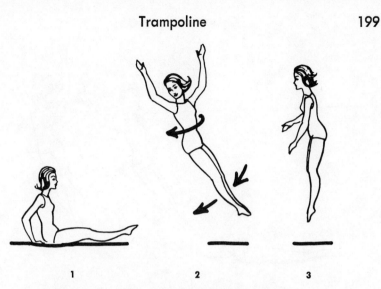

1   2   3

Fig. 7–9. Seat drop half twist to stand.

TEACHING TECHNIQUE. Before trying the seat drop half twist to feet the performer should do a quarter twist several times and end facing the side of the trampoline.

4. Full Pirouette. The full pirouette is a 360 degree twist or turn in a vertical position. It is executed in the same way as the half pirouette described in Routine I. The half pirouette is a lead-up stunt. More twist has to be started as the performer rebounds from the bed than in the half pirouette and the arms must remain over the head, in extension of the long axis of the body, a little longer. It is very important to keep the head erect. If the eyes look down at the bed before the twist is completed, it usually brings about a bending at the waist and this in turn results in an off-balance landing. The entire body must remain vertical throughout the stunt. The foot landing following the full pirouette is the sixth contact with the bed in this routine.

5. Seat Drop Half Twist to Seat Drop (Swivel-Hips) (Fig. 7–10). Following the pirouette another seat drop is executed (seventh contact). The swivel hips is actually a half pirouette done from seat to seat rather than from feet to feet. On the rebound from the seat drop (1) the arms push off the bed and lift above the head, the head and upper body start to twist to the left (or right) with the head looking over the left shoulder (2), the legs are pulled back directly underneath the body to a vertical position (3). The twist continues and the legs are raised forward again (4), and the stunt is completed in another seat drop position (5) (eighth contact).

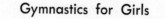

Fig. 7–10.   **Seat drop half twist to seat drop (swivel hips).**

TEACHING TECHNIQUES. The first lead-up stunt is a seat drop quarter twist to a stand on the bed facing the side of the trampoline. The next is a seat drop half twist to a stand facing the opposite direction. This stunt has already been described earlier in this routine. The most common mistake in learning the swivel hips is to swing the legs around to the side in a horizontal plane rather than to lower them to a vertical position. By using these two lead-up stunts this mistake will never develop.

Fig. 7–10.   Continued.

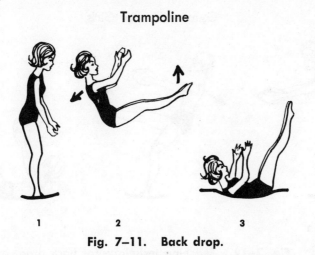

Fig. 7–11.   Back drop.

6. Back Drop (Fig. 7–11). The performer returns to the feet (ninth contact) following the seat drop half twist to seat drop (1). The last stunt in the routine is the back drop. On the rebound from the bed the performer leans backward and raises the legs forward (2). The landing on the bed is on the flat of the back from the shoulder blades to the buttocks. The legs should be straight and form an angle of 60 to 80 degrees with the bed of the trampoline. The head should be forward with the chin almost on the chest and the arms out to the side for balance (3). The elbows should be kept off the bed. It is a common mistake to drop the arms back to protect oneself. This does not aid in any way and usually results in skinned elbows. Because the legs are in front of the contact point on the landing, as the performer rebounds from the bed the weight of the legs will help turn the body forward and

Fig. 7–11.   Continued.

1   2   3

Fig. 7–12. Teaching technique for back drop.

bring the performer back to her feet. A little movement of the hips forward will also facilitate a return to the feet (4, 5). The back drop landing is the tenth bed contact and the return to the feet the eleventh contact in this routine.

TEACHING TECHNIQUES (Fig. 7–12). The performer should first become familiar with the landing position by assuming this position on the bed of the trampoline. The next step is to stand on the bed of the trampoline and hold an imaginary football at arms length in front of the body (1). One leg should be raised as if to kick this football and at the same time the performer should lean backward (2). Just as the balance is lost the other leg should push slightly off the bed and be raised to the same position as the kicking leg. The arms continue to hold the imaginary football out in front of the body on the landing so that the elbows do not get in the way (3). The next step is to try the stunt with both legs being raised together from a stand rather than a bounce.

III. INTERMEDIATE ROUTINE IN DETAIL

1. Half Twist to Back Drop (Fig. 7–13). This stunt starts as if the performer is going to do a front drop (1), but in the air the left hand is thrown across the chest and the head turned to the right to look up at the ceiling (2). As the half twist is completed the legs are raised and the performer lands in a regular back drop position (3) (first contact).

TEACHING TECHNIQUES. Work into the stunt gradually. Start by standing on the bed falling forward and twisting on the way

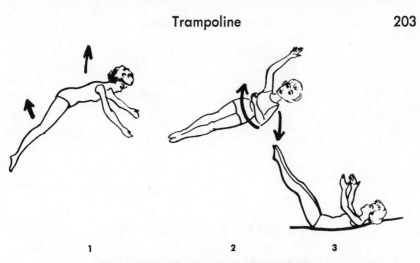

Fig. 7–13. Half twist to back drop.

down while the feet are still in contact with the bed. Next do the stunt with a very low bounce.

2. Half Twist to Feet (Fig. 7–14). As the performer rebounds from the bed after the back drop landing (1), the left arm is thrown across the chest and the right arm is pulled back and in close to the right side of the body. The head turns to the right so that the face looks back toward the bed (2). The performer should get the

Fig. 7–14. Half twist to feet.

feeling of lifting the hips and rolling them over (3). The landing is on the feet facing the opposite direction (4) (second contact). A common mistake is to twist too soon before rebounding from the bed. The half twist can be done in this way, but the landing will be dead and it will be impossible to bounce out of it so that the next stunt can be accomplished.

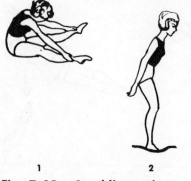

1   2

Fig. 7–15.   Straddle touch toes.

3. Straddle Touch Toes (Fig. 7–15).   This is just another leap or pose in the air. It adds beauty and height to this routine that is composed largely of stunts that are done quite close to the bed. The performer should spring hard into the air following the back drop half twist to feet. At the height of the bounce the legs are raised horizontally forward and spread wide apart. The trunk leans slightly forward and the arms reach for the toes (1). The legs are quickly lowered from this position to a regular vertical landing position (2) (third contact).

4. Front Drop Half Turn Table to Front Drop (Fig. 7–16).   These two front drops are the fourth and fifth contacts with the bed in this routine. The front drop has been described in Routine I. From the front drop landing the hands and forearms push to the right and the head moves vigorously to the left (1). The turn table is started with this push in the opposite direction from the intended movement while the body is straight. It is a common mistake to raise the head too high and look over the shoulder rather than to look at the upper arm. As the performer rebounds from the bed, the legs

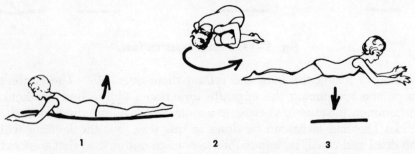

1   2   3

Fig. 7–16.   Front drop half turn table to front drop.

are tucked (or piked) thus shortening the body (2). This results in an increase in the speed of the turning motion. As the half turn-table is completed, the body is stretched for another regular front drop landing (3). From the second front drop the performer should rebound back to the feet (sixth contact).

TEACHING TECHNIQUES. The turn table can first be tried from a hand-knee drop to another hand-knee drop. This lead up is not necessary for most girls, however, as once a front drop is mastered the performer is ready to try the turn table without lead up stunts.

5. Back Drop to Front Drop (Fig. 7–17). These are the seventh and eighth contacts with the bed in this routine. Both stunts have been described previously, but the movement between the two is

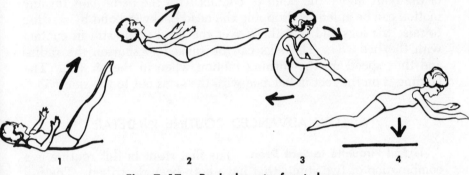

Fig. 7–17. Back drop to front drop.

new. From the back drop landing (1) the performer should get a kipping motion from the legs. This is done by extending them forcefully upward and forward at the time of rebound from the bed (2). The legs are drawn back under the body in the air (3). When the body reaches the horizontal position, the legs are stretched backward to a regular front drop landing (4). From this landing the performer rebounds to her feet (ninth contact).

TEACHING TECHNIQUES. This movement should be practiced from the back drop to a hand-knee drop at first.

6. Back Drop Pull-Over to Feet (Fig. 7–18). The performer starts as if going into a regular back drop (1) but does not raise the feet as high. The landing is on the small of the back or the point of the buttocks with the legs at about a 30 degree angle with the bed. The upper back should be slightly off the bed and the head forward. The arms should be out to the side well off the bed (2). As the performer rebounds from the bed, there is a natural tendency to turn over backward as the center of gravity is located in the upper part

Fig. 7–18.   Back drop pull-over to feet.

of the body above the point of contact with the bed. This turning motion can be aided by dropping the head backward and by starting to raise the legs and pull them over the head while still in contact with the bed (3). The legs can be tucked to shorten the radius and thus speed up the turning motion when in the air (4). The landing is on the feet in balance with the arms out to the side (5).

IV. LOW ADVANCED ROUTINE IN DETAIL

1. Full Pirouette to Seat Drop.   The first stunt in this routine is a combination of two stunts that have both been described. The full pirouette is done exactly the same as in Routine II except the landing is on the seat rather than on the feet. After the pirouette has been completed but before the feet contact the bed, the legs are raised forward for the seat drop landing as described in the first routine (contact one).

2. Seat Drop Full Twist to Seat Drop (Fig. 7–19). Before completely rebounding from the seat drop position, the performer starts the twist in the desired direction by pushing with the hands and

Fig. 7–19.   Seat drop full twist to seat drop.

turning the head and trunk slightly (1). The performer then leans backward from the waist so that the trunk and legs form a straight line almost parallel to the surface of the trampoline. One arm is thrown across the chest and the other backward and close to the side of the body. The head and upper body continue to twist in the direction started (2). In this position, with the body straight and the radius very short around the long axis, the twist is easy to complete. As it is completed the trunk is raised to an almost vertical position for the second seat drop landing (3) (second contact). In this stunt the feet and legs point toward the same end of the trampoline, parallel to the side of the bed throughout the entire movement.

TEACHING TECHNIQUES. A leadup stunt that can be used is a seat drop half twist to stomach drop. This teaches the performer to lean the upper body backward during the twist.

3. Back Drop Half Twist to Back Drop (Cradle) (Fig. 7–20). This stunt is a combination of two stunts that have already been explained in Routine III, the back drop to front drop and the half twist to back drop. Following the seat drop full twist to seat drop the performer comes back to her feet (third contact). She must learn to "dig-in" hard and use leg power to regain a reasonable amount

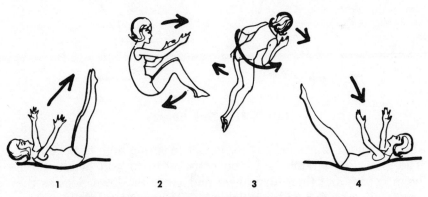

Fig. 7–20. Back drop half twist to back drop.

of height after the seat full twist to seat, which is a stunt that ends quite low. The next bed contact (fourth) is a regular back drop landing (1). The cradle starts from this position. The motion is exactly the same as if the performer is going to go from the back drop to a front drop (2). When the bed can be seen, the twist starts in the air as described in the half twist to back drop (3). The landing is in a regular back drop landing facing the opposite direction from the first back drop (4) (fifth contact).

TEACHING TECHNIQUES. Learn the two lead-up stunts mentioned before attempting the cradle.

4. Back Drop Half Twist to Feet. In order to get back to the feet after the cradle a half twist is executed. This move has already been explained in routine III. The foot landing is the sixth contact with the bed in this routine.

5. Tuck Bounce (Fig. 7–21). The performer will undoubtedly have lost most of her height at this point in the routine. The tuck bounce is designed to help regain height and to give some preliminary practice for the stunt which is to follow it. The performer

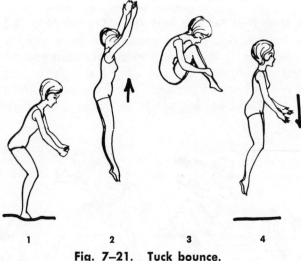

Fig. 7–21. Tuck bounce.

should "dig-in" hard and use leg power to spring high in the air (1). The arms first stretch high above the head to add height to the bounce (2), and then they lower and grasp the lower legs as they are drawn up into a tuck position (3). This position is held momentarily and then the body is stretched again for the next landing on the feet (4) (seventh contact).

6. Back Somersault (Back Flip) (Fig. 7–22). The stunts taught up to this point have been reasonably safe to learn. Only one has involved a position in which the head is below the rest of the body. It must be impressed upon all students that the "back flip," or for that matter any stunt that involves the body being upside down in

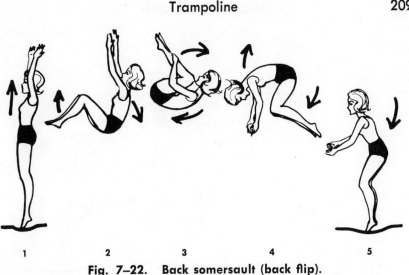

1   2   3   4   5

Fig. 7–22.   Back somersault (back flip).

the air, is potentially very dangerous and unless safety rules are followed serious accidents might occur. Most of the really active students in a physical education class are overly anxious to learn a "flip." The instructor should not scare these students but rather caution them. Most girls in a physical education class are capable of learning a back somersault on the trampoline.

As the performer rebounds from the bed, the arms reach in the normal way but possibly a little harder and a little higher so that they finish almost straight above the head. Before the feet leave the bed the rotation for the somersault is started by lifting the chest or arching the upper body slightly (1). At this point the hips must remain forward so that the center of gravity is almost above the feet or takeoff point. After the feet leave the bed, the head is dropped backward and the knees are pulled up toward the chest in a tuck position (2). The backward somersault, which was started by the slight chest lift which placed the head and upper body behind, and the hips slightly ahead of, the center of gravity, will speed up as the radius is shortened by pulling up the knees. As the legs reach the arms, the hands can grasp the shins, but this is not necessary (3). About half way through the somersault, if the head is back, the performer should be able to see the bed of the trampoline. Shortly after the halfway point in the somersault the tuck is gradually opened up (4) ready for the landing (5) (eighth contact).

TEACHING TECHNIQUES. Some instructors prefer to teach what is commonly called a "trampoline back" because it is easier for most

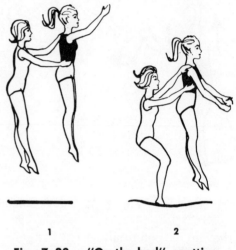

1   2

Fig. 7–23. "On-the-bed" spotting.

students than the somersault described above. In the "trampoline back" the head and upper body lean back much more than in the tuck back somersault. This would result in a traveling back somersault if the hips weren't kept well forward over the center of gravity. The hips thrust forward as well as upward during the first part of this type of somersault. After the takeoff the knees are drawn up a little, but this movement is not as pronounced as in the tuck back. Whatever method is taught first, the back somersault should certainly be learned completely before an attempt is made to put it in a routine. Several controlled preliminary bounces of medium height should be used before each practice trial.

The two most common mistakes made by those learning the back somersault are: one, on the takeoff bounce the feet are thrust forward; two, the upper body leans too far backward. Both of these mistakes result in a low traveling back somersault because the center of gravity is behind the feet on the takeoff. Traveling back somersaults can usually be corrected by moving the performer back on the bed and forcing her to start the somersault with only about three feet of bed behind her. Most performers soon learn to move forward or "gain" when presented with this situation. This technique can *not* be used unless an overhead belt is available.

SPOTTING. There are three types of spotting that can be successfully used. "On the bed" spotting can be used by men in-

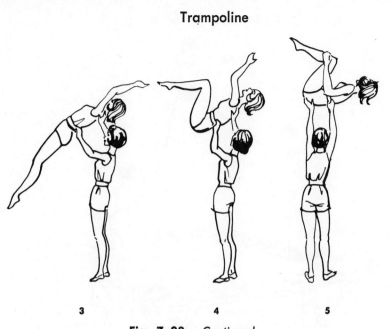

3   4   5

Fig. 7–23. *Continued.*

structors for all except the very heavy students. When working with beginners, women teachers should only attempt to use this method of spotting if they are exceptionally strong or if the performer is very small. All women should know this method, however, because it is normally used as a transition between a belt spot and the unaided performance of the somersault. In "on the bed" spotting (Fig. 7–23) the instructor bounces with the performer. One hand grasps a rope, towel, or the top of the performers shorts and the other is free to help spin or support the performer in one way or another (1). The spotter usually counts 1, 2, 3, and on three kills her bounce so that her feet remain on the trampoline (2). The spotter should practice this preliminary technique before attempting to spot a somersault. The first step in teaching a back somersault by the "on the bed" spotting technique is to hold the towel around the waist with the left hand and use the right hand to support the upper back while the performer reaches with the arms and leans the head and upper body backward (3). The spotter momentarily supports the performer's weight in the air but tips her back to land on her feet. The next step is exactly the same except the performer draws her knees up to her chest as she leans back on the spotter's hand (4). In the next step the spotter changes hands and grasps the towel that is wrapped around the waist with the right hand and uses the left hand under the hips of the performer to help spin her

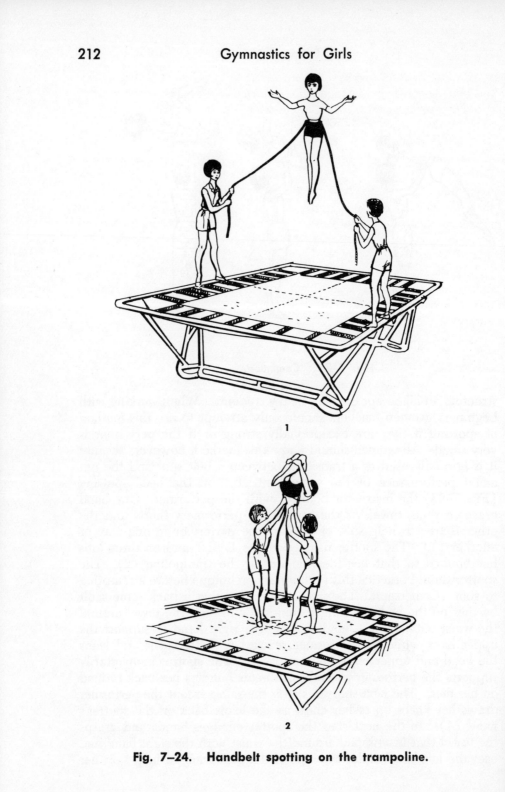

Fig. 7–24.   Handbelt spotting on the trampoline.

as she attempts the complete somersault (5). The last step in "on the bed" spotting is to stand on the frame of the trampoline and as the performer leaves the bed to execute the somersault step quickly onto the bed ready to give aid if necessary.

A hand belt (Fig. 7–24), held by spotters standing on the frame on both sides of the trampoline, can be used to spot a back somersault (1). One of the spotters should count 1, 2, 3, and, as the performer leaves the bed on the third bounce to execute the somersault, both spotters step quickly onto the bed and slide their hands along the rope close to the waist of the performer ready to support her weight (2). This method is not a good substitute for the overhead belt method.

The only good method of spotting back somersaults on the trampoline, if the performers are large or if the teacher is rather small, is to use a belt suspended from the ceiling by ropes that run through pulleys (Fig. 7–25). The distance between the pulleys should be about the same as the height from the trampoline to the beam on which the pulleys are fastened. This overhead spotting rig can be easily installed by the teacher or maintenance man.

When using one of these overhead spotting belts, the spotter should keep the ropes taut as the performer bounces up and down. This involves considerable arm movement on the part of the spotter. The usual technique is to grasp the rope firmly with one hand and pull down as the performer bounces in the air and then relax and

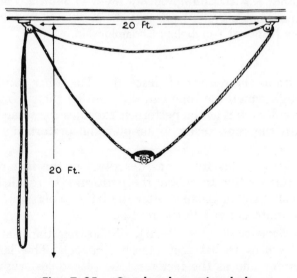

Fig. 7–25. Overhead spotting belt.

Barbara Gallaher Performing a Tuck Back Somersault During the 1962 National A.A.U. Championship Meet in Seattle. Barbara has been National Tumbling Champion seven times, the last time in 1962. She also won the National Trampoline Championship in 1961.

raise the arm as the performer descends. The other hand forms an "eye" through which the rope can slide during the performer's preliminary bounces, but as the performer executes the somersault both hands grasp the rope ready to support the performer's weight if necessary.

7. Seat Drop. This stunt was described in the first routine. It is used in this routine to enable the performer to regain control in case she is slightly off balance after the back somersault. This seat drop is the ninth contact in the routine.

8. Front Somersault (Fig. 7–26). Following the seat drop the performer returns to her feet (tenth contact). This landing is a very important one as the feet must be placed just right so as to obtain the correct position for the takeoff for the front somersault.

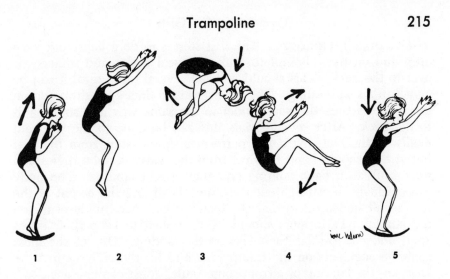

Fig. 7–26. Front somersault.

The hips should be slightly behind the center of gravity and the body slightly piked so that the head is in front of the center of gravity. The arms should be bent with the elbows close to the side and the hands about shoulder height (1). In the air the arms reach up and the head starts forward (2). The arms continue their motion forward, the head is tucked onto the chest, and the legs are drawn up into a tuck position. The hands usually grasp the shins in this tuck position (3). The performer must "time" the spin of the somersault and open out at the right time (4) for a controlled landing in an upright position (5) (eleventh contact). The performer can't see the bed on the landing of the front somersault as she can in the back somersault. Although the front somersault seems easier for most performers at first, it is harder to get a balanced landing after the front somersault than after the back flip. As it is very difficult to land well enough to be able to do another stunt immediately following, the front somersault is seldom used in trampoline routines unless used as the last stunt. Even though it is not used very much in routines, it is essential for a performer to learn the front somersault if she wants to continue with advanced trampoline work, as the same movement is used in several of the more advanced stunts.

SPOTTING. The spotter standing around the trampoline, especially the one on the end the performer is facing, should watch carefully in case the performer bounces off the bed. Apart from this, spotting is not commonly used for the front somersault. If proper progression is followed, it is not necessary to help the performer.

TEACHING TECHNIQUES. The first step is to do a hand and knee drop and on the rebound to tuck the head under and somersault over to the back. This should be tried several times until it can be ended in a seat landing. The next step is to do a knee drop and on the rebound tuck the head under in the same way and somersault to the back. After several trials this can be done to the seat and finally to the feet. Next the performer should start from the feet but at first should bend forward from the waist at right angles and somersault to a back landing and then a seat landing. The body can gradually be straightened on the takeoff and the height of the somersault increased so that the feet can be placed underneath on the landing. Performers should be cautioned to keep their knees apart and not to relax their legs on the landing. One of the most common accidents on the trampoline is to hit the chin against the knees on the landing of a front somersault. Most of these accidents can be prevented if the performers are warned ahead of time.

V. ADVANCED ROUTINE IN DETAIL

1. Layout Back Somersault (Fig. 7–27). A "layout" somersault is an arched body somersault. More backward spin has to be started off the bed than in a regular back somersault because the legs are not tucked to shorten the radius and thus speed up the spin. This means that the chest and upper body have to be leaned back a little more than in the tuck back somersault. This in turn means the hips have to be carried further forward so that the center of gravity is not too far behind the feet. If the center of gravity does get too far behind the feet, the somersault will be low and the

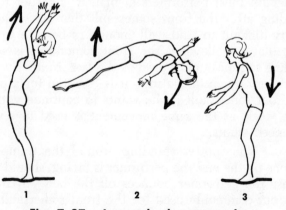

Fig. 7–27.   Layout back somersault.

performer will travel backward. On the takeoff, therefore, the hips are well forward, the upper body and head are well back, and the arms are stretched above the head (1). In the air the arms move in a smooth pulling motion from a position above the head to one out to the side of the body, the head pulls hard backward, the chest and the stomach thrust well forward to give an arch to the body, and the legs trail straight and together behind the upper body (2). As the somersault is completed, the head returns to an erect or maybe a slightly forward position and the body pikes slightly ready for the landing (3) (first contact).

TEACHING TECHNIQUES. Even though the regular back somersault has been learned, the performer will probably have to get back into the belt to learn the layout back. The same teaching techniques and spotting techniques should be used in teaching this somersault.

2. Baroni (Fig. 7–28). The baroni is a half-twisting front somersault in a pike position. It is very similar to the roundoff in tumbling except that it is done without resting the weight on the hands. To present the baroni as described here it must be assumed that the teacher is acquainted with the roundoff and that the student has at least partially learned this stunt on the tumbling mats.

The takeoff position is the same as for the front somersault. The body should be slightly piked so that the hips are behind and the head and upper body in front of the center of gravity. The arms are bent so that the elbows are down and close to the side of the body and the hands are about shoulder height (1). The twisting motion

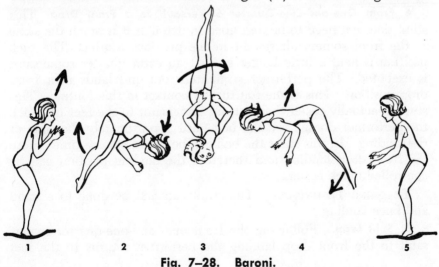

1   2   3   4   5

Fig. 7–28. Baroni.

is started slightly before the performer leaves the bed by turning the head and upper body slightly to the side. During the upward flight the arms reach up and then forward and the hips lift directly up behind the body (2). As the performer reaches maximum height, the body is straightened and the legs pass directly over the head. A quarter twist has been completed at this point (3). On the way down the body is piked again and the second quarter twist is executed (4). The landing should be in approximately the same position as the takeoff (5) (second contact).

SPOTTING. This stunt can be spotted in an overhead belt. A twisting belt makes it easier to spot the performer, but a regular belt can be used if the performer twists halfway round before attempting the stunt so that she unwinds the ropes as the stunt is done. Usually the stunt is learned without spotting by following the teaching techniques outlined below.

TEACHING TECHNIQUES. The first step in learning the baroni is to do a roundoff from a knee landing to a knee landing with the hands touching the bed in between the two landings. The feet must go directly over the head and not around to the side. The eyes can be focused on the bed of the trampoline throughout this lead up drill and, for that matter, while the baroni itself is executed. The next step is to do a two-foot roundoff from feet to hands to feet. The final step is to try the complete stunt.

3. Back Somersault. The back somersault was taught in Routine IV. The landing on this stunt is the third contact with the bed in this routine.

4. Front One-and-One-Quarter Somersault to a Front Drop. This stunt does not need to be described in detail as it is much the same as the front somersault taught in the previous routine. The tuck position is held a little longer so that an extra quarter somersault is executed. The performer straightens out and lands in a front drop position. This is the fourth bed contact in this routine. This stunt is actually easier than a front somersault to the feet in which the performer doesn't see the bed until approximately the time of the landing. In this stunt the bed can be seen for some time before the front drop landing and therefore the landing position can be controlled much easier.

TEACHING TECHNIQUES. The stunt can first be done to a hand and knee landing.

5. Split Leap. Following the front one- and-one-quarter somersault to the front drop landing the performer returns to the feet (fifth contact). The bounce will be quite low at this point in the routine so it is necessary to dig in hard and use leg power to obtain sufficient height for the next stunt. The split leap is just a high bounce in the air in which one leg is raised forward and one backward in a split position. The split position should be reached at the height of the bounce and then the legs rapidly lowered ready for the next landing on the feet (sixth contact).

6. Three-Quarter Back Somersault to Front Drop. A three-quarter back somersault is a slow, lazy layout back somersault done to a stomach landing rather than to the feet. The same techniques that were used for the layout somersault apply to this stunt. The take-off position and position in the air during the first part of the somersault is much the same as in the layout somersault. Less chest lift and less head and arm pull are used so that only three quarters of a somersault are executed. The landing (seventh contact) is in a front drop position.

TEACHING TECHNIQUES. Until the performer learns to adjust her position in the air and land in a good front drop position it is much safer for her to land in a hand-knee drop.

7. Stag Leap. The previous stunt ends in a stomach landing on the trampoline. From this position the performer rebounds back to her feet (eighth contact). The next stunt is a stag leap which was described in the very first routine. It is used here to give the performer an opportunity to increase the height of her bounce so that it is high enough for the stunt that follows. Stunts such as this are not used in boys' trampoline work but are excellent for girls as they add beauty and grace to the exercise. The stag leap is finished on the feet (ninth contact).

8. Back One-and-One-Quarter Somersault Pull-Over to Feet (Fig. 7-29). This is a combination of two stunts—the back somersault (1) (2) and the back drop pull-over to feet. The back somersault is overspun so that the feet miss the bed (3). The tuck position in the somersault must be held longer than for a regular back somersault. The landing is on the small of the back (4). From this position the pull-over is executed exactly as described in Routine III which was also finished with a pull-over (5) (6). The landing on the back and the landing on the feet, after the pull-over, are the tenth and eleventh bed contacts in this routine.

TEACHING TECHNIQUES. The tuck back somersault should be completely mastered before this stunt is attempted. The next step is to land in a seat drop landing. This requires very little extra

Fig. 7–29. Back one-and-one-quarter somersault pull-over to feet.

spin but does give the idea of going slightly beyond a foot landing. The next step is to land on the back but to rebound back to the feet as in a regular back drop instead of pulling over to the feet.

OTHER ADVANCED STUNTS

There are several more advanced stunts that can be learned by the well-coordinated and daring high school or college girl. Once learned these stunts can be inserted into the routines included in this chapter or used as a part of new routines composed by the individual performer.

1. Cody (Fig. 7–30). The cody is a back somersault done from a stomach landing. It can be started from a regular front drop,

Fig. 7–30. Cody.

but it is usually done after a three-quarter back somersault. The landing at the start of the stunt is the same as a front drop except the knees are flexed so that the feet are off the bed (1). The somersault is started by pushing from the bed with the hands and lifting with the head and upper body (2). As the performer rebounds off the bed, the upper body rebounds faster than the legs and lower body and thus starts the backward somersault (3). As the body leaves the bed, the knees are drawn up to the chest into a tight tuck (4). The radius is thus shortened and the rotation of the somersault speeds up. The performer opens out of the tuck for the landing (5).

SPOTTING. The cody can be spotted with an overhead spotting belt or with a hand spot. In the hand spotting method the spotter stands on the frame of the trampoline and, as the performer rebounds from the bed, quickly steps on and helps to turn the performer over to her feet. The spotter must be careful not to step onto the bed until the performer is completely clear of the bed.

TEACHING TECHNIQUES. The performer should master a front drop to a back drop before trying the cody. She should also be able to do a good tightly tucked back somersault.

2. Full Twisting Back Somersault (Fig. 7–31). The full twisting back somersault starts much like a layout back somersault. The arms lift almost straight above the head with the hands a little wider apart than the shoulders. The upper body leans well back, but the hips are kept forward so that the center of gravity is approximately above the feet (1). Backward twists are usually started before the feet leave the bed, although this is not the only method that can be used. The twist is started with the upper body

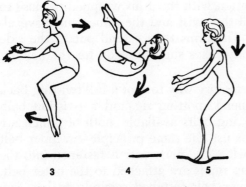

3   4   5

Fig. 7–30. *Continued.*

Fig. 7–31.   Full twisting back somersault.

by turning the head, shoulders, and trunk slightly in the desired direction while the feet are still in contact with the bed. The feet can also help initiate the twist by pushing sideways on the bed on the takeoff. The twisting motion started on the bed will continue in the air especially if the body is kept straight to facilitate the twist (2). The arm motion is very important. Both arms lift above the head in a fairly wide position and then in the air are wrapped in close against the chest to shorten the radius around the twisting axis and thereby speed up the twist. In a twist to the left, the right arm is thrown across the front of the body in a straight position and then the elbow bends and the arm folds in close to the chest. The left arm throws backward with the elbow bending in close to the side (3). The straight body position with the arms wrapped in close to the chest is maintained until the twist and the somersault have almost been completed (4). The arms then extend out to the side to stop the twist and the body pikes slightly ready for the landing (5, 6).

Spotting. The only satisfactory way to spot a full twisting back somersault is with an overhead spotting rig and a twisting belt. There are two kinds of twisting belts available, both of which are very satisfactory. Both types use the same principle—an inner belt that spins within an outer belt. The performer is fastened into the inner belt and the supporting ropes are attached to the outer belt. The performer, with the inner belt fastened securely to her, can

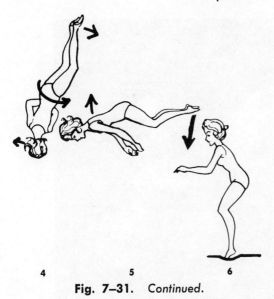

4   5   6

Fig. 7–31. *Continued.*

twist freely within the outer belt which is prevented from twisting
by the supporting ropes. Figure 7–32a shows a twisting belt with
an inner belt that spins within the outer belt on a roller bearing
track. Figure 7–32b shows another type with an inner plastic belt
that spins within an outer metal belt. Both inner and outer belts
have very smooth surfaces that offer little resistance as they slide

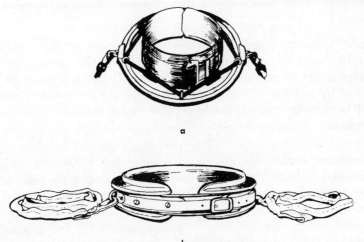

a

b

Fig. 7–32. Twisting belts.

Barbara Gallaher Performing a Double Twisting Back Somersault on the Trampoline. Note how close her arms are to her body during the twist. (See photo on page 214 for more information about Miss Gallaher.)

on one another. Some very experienced spotters can spot a full twist by hand by bouncing on the bed with the performer. This method is not recommended for most teachers. A regular belt can be used by turning 360 degrees and wrapping the ropes around the waist before the stunt is started. The ropes unwind as the twist is executed.

TEACHING TECHNIQUES. The performer should be able to do a good layout back somersault and a good full pirouette before attempting a full twisting back somersault. Most girls take far too many preliminary bounces before trying the twist. A good part of each practice session should be spent trying the twist after just one preliminary bounce at a very low height. It helps some performers to think about thrusting the right hip forward when trying to twist to the left.

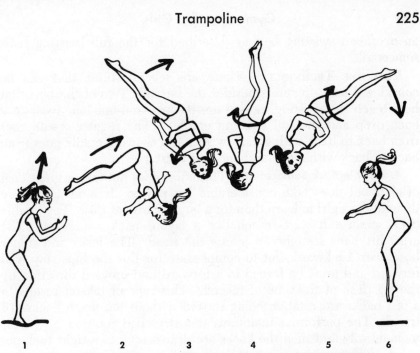

Fig. 7–33. Front one-and-one-half twisting somersault.

3. Front One-and-One-Half Twisting Somersault (Fig. 7–33). The front somersault with a one-and-one-half twist is started much the same as a baroni. On the takeoff the body is in a slight pike position with the hips behind and the head and upper body in front of the feet (1). The feet push up and back on the takeoff and the hips lift hard upward and backward. The arms also lift upward during this part of the stunt. About the time maximum height has been reached the body should be upside down in a sharp pike position with the arms stretched out to the side of the body and the head back with the eyes focused on the bed (2). From this position the twist starts. If the twist is to the left, the right arm is thrown vigorously across the front of the body with the hand almost brushing the ankle and the left elbow is thrown backward. The head is also turned vigorously to the left and looks over the left shoulder. The body then straightens and both arms pull in close to the chest so that the radius around the longitudinal axis is as short as possible during the twist (3) (4). The twist is completed with the body straight (5). As the one-and-one-half twist is completed, the arms move out away from the body and the hips are slightly flexed so that the landing will be in a slight pike position (6).

SPOTTING. The only satisfactory way to spot this stunt is with an overhead twisting belt as described for the full twisting back somersault.

TEACHING TECHNIQUES.   There are several stunts that can be considered lead up stunts besides the baroni. Two of the best that help teach the twisting motion are the one-and-one-half twist to a back drop and the full twisting cradle. (The regular cradle goes from back to back with a half twist; a full twisting cradle goes from back to back with a one-and-one-half twist.)

4. Double Back Somersault.   This stunt does not take a great deal of skill but does take considerable leg power. It is usually more difficult for a girl to learn than for a boy because of this. The double back somersault starts much like a layout back somersault. The arms lift hard straight up above the head. The head and upper body lean backward, but to compensate for this the hips stay well forward and must be forced in a forward and upward direction by the leg push at the time of takeoff. This type of takeoff results in a fast backward rotation being started without too much backward travel. The performer maintains this stretched position in the air momentarily and then the knees are drawn up into a tight tuck position. This position is maintained until the double somersault has been almost completed at which time the tuck is opened for the landing. The opening of the tuck and the timing of the landing must be done by "feel" as the rotation is too fast for the performer to "see" where she is until after the rotation has been slowed down by opening the tuck.

SPOTTING.   An overhead spotting rig should be used to teach this stunt.

TEACHING TECHNIQUES.   Before starting on the double back the performer should be able to do high tuck and high layout back somersaults in good control. There is a natural tendency to start to open the tuck after the first revolution so the performer should be told to make a conscious effort to pull in the legs a little tighter at this time. Three things should be emphasized in a double back somersault:

1. A high bounce to give more time in the air.
2. A takeoff that gets lots of backward rotation started.
3. A tight tuck after the rotation has been started.

A girl who is not able to complete the double somersault must be lacking in one or more of these things.

8

Competitive Gymnastics

DIGEST OF RULES

A complete set of rules can be obtained from the Amateur
Athletic Union, New York, New York; or the Division of Girls' and
Women's Sports of the American Association for Health, Physical
Education and Recreation, Washington, D.C. The Gymnastic
Guide and Rule Book, published by the A.A.U., also includes in-
formation from various International Gymnastic Federation Pub-
lications (F.I.G.) released by the women's international technical
committee. The D.G.W.S. Gymnastic Guide published by the
A.A.H.P.E.R. includes considerable gymnastic information as well
as the rules adopted by this organization.

The Amateur Athletic Union at this time is the governing body
for women's open gymnastic competition in the United States. The
Division of Girls' and Women's sports establishes policies, procedures, and standards for competition for teachers and leaders
actively engaged in the physical education profession. These organizations are playing an important part in the rapid development
of girls' and women's gymnastics in the United States.

Another organization called the United States Gymnastic Federation will be formed in the near future. This organization is re-
ceiving considerable support from the National Collegiate Athletic
Association, other national gymnastic groups, and by the coaches
themselves. At this time it is difficult to say what its exact func-
tion and services will be.

The following few pages are a digest, with comment and inter-
pretation, of the rules of the I.G.F. and the A.A.U. of the U.S. The
D.G.W.S. rules were not available at the time of writing.

The rules state that:

1. Gymnastics for women should include elements of skill, grace, and rhythm rather than strength.
2. The physique of women should determine the nature of the movement.
3. Health shall be protected.

There are three levels or grades of competition held in most local A.A.U. Associations (districts)—Novice, Junior, and Senior. Competitors must be at least fifteen years of age to compete in championship meets. A girl can place herself at whatever level she wishes. Once she has won a first, second, or third place in any event in the Novice Division she must move up to the Junior Division in that event. If she wins a first place in any event in the Junior Division, she must move up to the Senior Division in that event.

There are no official team championship awards made in women's competition, but team awards are unofficially made to the organization scoring the highest number of points for all events contested as follows: international events (in which both a compulsory and optional exercise are required), 7 points for first, 5 for second, 4 for third, 3 for fourth, 2 for fifth, and 1 point for sixth; special events (in which only an optional exercise is required), $3\frac{1}{2}$ points for first, $2\frac{1}{2}$ points for second, 2 for third, $1\frac{1}{2}$ for fourth, 1 for fifth, and $\frac{1}{2}$ point for sixth. There must be at least two contestants scoring points for a team in order for the team to be considered for a championship.

The list of approved events for district and national meets are:

International Events	Special Events
1. Floor exercise	1. Tumbling
2. Uneven parallel bars	2. Rebound tumbling
3. Balance beam	(trampoline)
4. Side horse vault	
5. All-around (consisting of 1–4)	

The normal procedure used to determine the winner in an event is to total the score obtained in the compulsory and optional exercises for the international events and to use just one score from an optional performance in the special events. Sometimes a second optional exercise is averaged with the compulsory and first optional score to determine individual winners in both the international and special events. (This is done in National Championship Meets.) The all-round winner is determined by adding the scores in compulsory and first optional exercises for all four international events (total of eight scores).

The order of events in a meet is determined by a meet committee and usually differs for each meet. Most of the compulsory work is held in one session and the optional in another. A two-session meet is sometimes held on two different days, but both sessions can be held on the same day. The meet committee usually selects the order in which competitors perform by drawing names out of a hat; however, no competitor must perform first in more than one event.

OFFICIALS

The general direction of a meet is assumed by the referee. She decides all matters not covered by the rules.

The judging in each event is done by six judges one of whom is appointed as superior judge. The superior judge sees that the five judges assigned to her event are in their proper places, alert, and attentive to the competition. She notifies the other judges of any variations in prescribed exercises. She calls for a consultation of judges after the first two competitors and may be consulted at any time by judges regarding any particular in connection with the competition. She scores each exercise for her own reference during consultations.

The scoring judges place themselves apart from each other so as to observe the general form of the competitor from different angles. Each judge, without consultation, except as specified in the rules, marks her score on her score sheet on a one-tenth basis, i.e. 9.2, 8.7, 7.8, etc., immediately after the completion of each performance. A score of ten is awarded for a perfect exercise.

The superior judge makes note of the five marking judges' scores. Of the five marks obtained by each contestant the highest mark and the lowest is eliminated and the average of the three remaining marks calculated. The spread between the highest and lowest mark of these three scores cannot exceed .3 of a point when the average score is 9.0 or higher, .5 of a point if they average between 8.0 and 8.95, or one point if they average below 8.0. (There is a mistake in the 1962–63 rule book regarding this maximum permissible range between the middle three scores.) If these limits are exceeded, the judges consult and change their scores to come within the required range.

The official score and results are kept by the scorekeepers, one of whom is appointed as chief scorer. The scorers record on official score sheets (see Appendix, pages 255–58) the mark of the five scoring judges and then cross out the highest and lowest. The three middle marks are then added and averaged (divided by three) to obtain the score for the exercise. If there are two or more identical high or low marks, only one of them is discarded. An average chart, including averages for numbers from .3 to 30.0, should be available for the scorekeepers. After obtaining the total of the three middle scores scorekeepers can refer to this total on the chart to get the average.

Timers are needed for floor exercises, balance beam, tumbling, and rebound tumbling. (Note: A timer is not needed for rebound tumbling if the present rules are modified as explained in Chapter 7.)

The announcer is a very important official at a gymnastic meet. Rather than just reporting what is happening, as in most athletic events, she is directly responsible for keeping the meet on schedule. More will be said about the duties of the announcer later in this chapter.

TYPES OF EXERCISES

When compulsory or required exercises are used, they must be executed exactly as described except that they may be wholly reversed from right to left. Single parts of an exercise may not be reversed.

Voluntary or optional exercises must include five difficult movements one of which should be rated extremely difficult. They must differ from the compulsory exercises. If movements included in the compulsory exercises are repeated in the optional, they are considered duplication and credit is not given for those movements. All skills requiring primarily strength or force are considered undesirable. Preference is given to exercises with movement.

Floor Exercises.   The duration of the exercise is from one minute to one minute and thirty seconds. The 12 meter by 12 meter area (40 feet by 40 feet) should be used in its entirety. The exercise must make use of the entire body, must contain artistically performed movements, leaps, balances, and poses and must be executed in a lively manner with change of pace and expression. There should be no held positions. (There is a mistake in the 1962–1963 rule book on this point. It incorrectly states that poses should be held for three seconds.) The voluntary exercise, like the required, must be accompanied by music and should harmonize with the music composition.

Balance Beam.   The duration of the exercise is from one and one-half to two minutes. It must be elegant, lively, put into action all parts of the body, and contain sitting and lying positions, running and walking steps, springs or jumps, turns and sustained positions, without letting the held positions predominate over the other components. Execution must be with sureness, suppleness, and expressiveness. Monotony of rhythm must be avoided.

Uneven Parallel Bars. Movements involving suspension from the hands and releases from the bars should predominate in the exercise. Supports should only be used as temporary positions. Balances are acceptable provided they are specially suited to the bars and are only held momentarily. Movements that are common in floor exercises and beam should be avoided. Only dismounts requiring a hand grip should be used.

Side Horse Vault. All vaults must be done with the hands placed on the horse. Two trials are permitted on the prescribed and two on the optional vault, but only the best trial of each is used in determining the competitors standing. The two voluntary attempts may differ. The difficulty rating of vaults is listed in the rules. Only listed vaults may be used.

Tumbling. The duration of the exercise is two minutes, in which a maximum of four trips down the mat may be performed. Only fast moving tumbling stunts should be used. Contortional or dance movements and balances are not considered tumbling stunts.

Rebound Tumbling (Trampoline). The exercise is composed of two sequences composed of a reasonable number of preparatory bounces and then a maximum of eight contacts with the bed in each sequence. The sequences are separated by a compulsory twenty-second rest period.

In the beam and uneven parallel bar events any gymnast can repeat, without loss of points, a compulsory exercise which she has carried out badly, provided she announces her intentions to the head judge before she has been scored. A reasonable rest time is permitted. Only the repeat performance is scored. In these two events, if a gymnast falls from the apparatus, she can complete her exercise with a penalty of one point per fall provided she remounts within three seconds. This applies to both the compulsory and optional exercises.

In floor exercises, tumbling, and rebound tumbling, exercises may not be repeated. A fall from the apparatus in rebound tumbling terminates the exercise.

JUDGING

A. Prescribed Exercises. In judging prescribed exercises only the execution and general impression are subject to evaluation. To insure the most accurate judging possible, prescribed exercises are divided into parts. Each part is given a value proportional to the difficulty of the part. A list of principal errors is also established with the corresponding penalties.

B. Voluntary Exercises. The ten points for the prescribed exercises are distributed as follows: 5 points—3 for difficulty, 2 for technical value; 5 points—2 for execution, 3 for general impression.

A voluntary exercise should contain five elements of difficulty, one element being extremely difficult. For each of those elements that are omitted the penalty is .6 of a point. If no difficult moves are included, the penalty is three points. There is no easy way for a judge to score difficulty. She must know what the difficult stunts are and be able to recognize them, and keep a count of them as the exercise is performed. A comprehensive list of stunts considered to be "difficulties" is contained in the rule book. They are listed separately for each event under the heading "International Grouping." From this international grouping of stunts it is up to the individual judge to determine the stunts that are "extremely difficult."

The technical value of an exercise is rated in many ways. All of the requirements listed previously for each event under "types of exercises" must be included to get a perfect score for technical value. Points are also deducted from this category: If the exercise resembles the compulsory; if there are unnecessary movements included; if the stunts, or combination of stunts, are of the wrong type for that particular event; or if the exercise is too short or too long (the uneven bar event should be composed of at least ten principal parts).

The two points for execution and three for general impression are very difficult to separate. The deductions for execution are quite specific, but the deductions for general impression are more subjective. Many judges consider these two things together and follow men's rules, which include a five-point category for execution and do not mention general impression. General impression indirectly is related to technical value, as the general impression would undoubtedly be lowered if the technical value of the exercise were low.

Deductions for execution are broken down into small, medium, and serious errors with deductions of .1 to .2, .3, to .5, and .5 and more respectively for the three divisions. Examples of small, medium, and serious errors are as follows:

> Small errors—head bowed, toes not pointed, arms slightly bent during supports, small interruptions in rhythm, and small step or slight jump upon dismounting.
> Medium errors—legs bent or widely spread, arms bent in hand-

stands, nonspecified slight bending of the torso, hands touching the ground on dismounts, or stiff movements instead of supple ones.

Serious errors—repeating a failed movement, falling on the pelvis or knees on dismounts, falling during an exercise, or coaches' aid during an exercise.

General impression includes such things as perfect technique in execution and ease of performance. The difficulty of the exercise should correspond to the capability of the competitor. An exercise which is executed with great effort or which is just barely mastered is severely penalized. A gymnast should complete her exercise with grace, precision, elegance, ease, and sureness to get full marks for general impression.

The rules contain many more specific deductions for various faults. Some of these apply only to certain events. Anyone interested in more detailed information about judging can refer to the rule book.

HOW TO JUDGE

The first step in good judging is to get a rule book and study it carefully. The second step is to practice, practice, practice. This does not necessarily have to be done in a competitive situation. A judge can evaluate performances at a team practice session and get considerable experience in this way.

The digest of the rules contained in this chapter gives practically all the information necessary for a judge except "how to judge." There are almost as many different methods of judging as there are judges, but only two methods that have proved successful will be presented in this chapter. Individual judges may modify one of these or use a combination of the two. Certainly every judge can, and should, develop techniques of her own that will help her do a better job. In both methods the performer starts with ten points and her mistakes and weaknesses are subtracted from ten to give her final score.

METHOD I

As the gymnast performs keep a record of her routine on a piece of scratch paper by using a type of short hand consisting of abbreviations, letters, symbols, etc. At first this sounds impossible but with practice a judge can record an entire exercise in this way. This should be done without taking the eyes off the performer. At the same time this is being done a record of the number of deductions (in tenths of points) for execution should be kept in the head. When the gymnast is through, the score for "execution" can be obtained by subtracting the total deductions from two points, the score for "difficulty" and "technical value" can be quickly figured from the routine that has been recorded on the scratch pad, and finally the score for "general impression" can be subjectively estimated after the other scores are recorded. The four scores are then totaled to give the final score.

METHOD II

Nothing is written down in this method. It therefore involves training the memory so that the routine can be recalled. A record of the "difficulties" are kept by extending the fingers of the left hand as the routine is performed. At the completion of the routine the score for difficulty can be quickly determined by counting the number of extended fingers. During the performance a tally is kept on a scratch pad of the number of deductions (in tenths of points) for execution. At the end of the routine the score for execution can be calculated by simple subtraction. The routine must be recalled to mind so that a score for technical value can be awarded. The score for general impression is subjectively estimated and then the four scores are totaled, as in method I, to give the final score.

It is much easier to judge expert performers than it is to judge novices. Experts usually include the required number of "difficulties" to obtain the maximum score and are careful to compose their routine so that it satisfies the "technical value" requirement. As top performers seldom have major deductions for "execution" or "general impression," it is relatively easy to keep account of the few tenths here and few tenths there that have to be deducted.

Many judges think that novices should not be judged as severely as advanced performers. Some think that the better performers in a meet, no matter what the level of performance, should be awarded scores between nine and ten. This makes gymnastic judging, which is subjective at its best, so subjective in nature that it becomes a guessing game. Until a more definite and objective method of judging the lower levels of performance is devised, everyone should be judged on the standards provided by the rules. This means that many scores for novice meets will be in the threes and fours and that the maximum score obtainable by a gymnast with no "difficulties" will be seven.

In some sections of the country the judges confer after the first performer and decide on a score. After that they award scores by comparing other performances with the first performance and deciding whether these other performances are ½, 1, or 1½ points or more better or worse than the first performance. This is a very subjective method of judging and is unfair to the gymnast. Judges will never become qualified if they judge in this way as they are not practicing the techniques involved in good judging. (Please do not confuse this method of judging with the simplified method, for classroom competition and intramural meets, recommended later in the chapter, in which one competitor is compared to another competitor rather than being awarded a score as provided by the rules. In this simplified judging method only two competitors are involved so a comparison is a much easier matter.)

COMPETITION IN PHYSICAL EDUCATION CLASSES

There are many forms of competition that can be used in physical education gymnastic classes to stimulate interest in the activity. Most of these suggestions can be used in beginning classes as well as in advanced classes. Some can be used throughout the class period as a part of the daily activity. Some are best when used at the end of the period during the last five or ten minutes. Some are appropriate for the whole class, some are best used within a single squad.

1. Put the best performer at the front of the line after the performance of each stunt. If a record is kept of the number of times a player has been at the head of the line, this form of competition becomes more interesting as a squad champion can be decided at the end of the class period. Good squad leaders are needed to make this technique work well.

2. Select the best performer in each squad to compete against the best performer in other squads. This competition could be in the performance of a single stunt rather than a routine. The technique does not have to be restricted to the best in the squad. The second best performer could be chosen from each squad to represent their squad in competition in another stunt, and still another person chosen to compete in a third stunt. If the best in each squad is chosen, however, a class champion can then be selected for each stunt. This adds interest to the competition.

3. Use check lists of stunts. Students compete to see who can accomplish the greatest number of stunts. Check lists can be of a

permanent type that are posted on the wall throughout the entire gymnastic unit or ones that are used for a single day, with a new list being introduced the next day.

4. Have a "record board" for such things as:

    a. number of pulls ups
    b. handwalking for distance (or handstand for time)
    c. number of consecutive swivel hips on the trampoline
    d. greatest distance from takeoff to landing on the straddle vault over the horse.

5. Have an "achievement board" with appropriate names given to the various levels of achievement. Those who accomplish the easiest list of stunts might be called the "shooting stars." Those who accomplish the next list the "junior varsity." The next level might be called the "varsity" and the top level the "professionals." There should be a bulletin board on which is displayed the names of the individuals who have reached the various levels of achievement.

6. Have a ladder tournament board for each event. Permit challenges at any time or designate certain days as challenge days. The teacher or a group of student judges can determine the winner and whether there should be a change in order on the ladder.

7. Hold tumbling relay races. Relays should only be held occasionally as sloppy execution often results from trying to hurry. They should be used with caution as certain stunts become very hazardous when done hurriedly. The type of relay usually used is to have the first girl in each line perform a certain stunt such as a cartwheel, a forward roll, or an animal walk down the row of mats and then run back and touch the next girl in line. A better type of relay is to have the first girl in each line run to a mat located at the other end of the gym, turn and face her squad, and then execute a single stunt, such as a headstand or a headspring, and then run back to touch the next girl. If the stunt is missed, penalties can be imposed such as running back backward, or hopping back on one leg. By making players run beyond the mat and turn before executing the stunt they are slowed down so that the stunt can be executed with a minimum of danger. By imposing a penalty if the stunt is missed proper execution is encouraged.

8. Play follow the leader in each squad. The leader performs a stunt and then everyone tries it. Those who miss are dropped from competition. The last girl left is the leader for the next game. A variation is to place the girls who miss at the end of the line rather than dropping them from the game. At the end of a certain time limit the girl directly behind the leader becomes the leader for the

next game. Players should be of approximately equal ability or this could be a dangerous game. Even with equal ability groups careful spotting is necessary.

9. Play "add on." The first girl performs a single stunt. The next girl does that stunt and one more. The third player adds one more and so on. This game is a test of memory as well as physical ability. Those who miss a stunt or forget the next stunt are dropped from competition. Those who are eliminated in these dropout games can be assigned as spotters or assigned to a designated practice area to practice the stunt missed. There are other techniques that can be used to make sure that no one is left out completely. Dropout games are fun, but the student that possesses little ability can be easily discouraged unless some provision is made for her after she has been dropped from competition.

10. One of the best forms of competition to use in a gymnastic class is team competition between two or more squads. The whole class does not have to be involved on the same day, but probably the most effective way to use this form of competition is to have the whole class compete during the last ten or fifteen minutes of each class period. This is much the same technique that is used in teaching other physical education activities—the first part of the period being devoted to practice of skills and lead-up drills and the last part of the period being devoted to "playing the game."

In gymnastic classes, if squads are about equal in ability, team competition can be held between squads. If squad assignments are made according to ability, as they should be, the class will have to be divided into teams of approximately equal ability for purposes of competition. Let us assume there are six teams in the class. In one class period two teams compete on the balance beam and then in tumbling. Two more teams compete on the trampoline and next in floor exercises. The last two teams compete in vaulting and uneven bars. The next class period teams are assigned to different events for competition.

It is not necessary to have five judges and official score keepers for this intraclass competition. One student official can serve as announcer, judge, and scorekeeper quite easily for each contest. In the hypothetical class mentioned above three contests are going on at the same time so three officials are needed. These officials might be squad leaders, the better performers in the class, or class members who are unable to take part in strenuous activity on that particular day.

Full length routines should not be used for this type of competition. In an event like the balance beam this would involve too much time. Either a short required or optional routine consisting of a mount, one or two stunts on the equipment, and a dismount can be used. In tumbling one trip down the mat, and in vaulting one vault, is sufficient.

The best way to determine the winner in intraclass competition is to match each girl against a girl from the other team. The competitors don't compete for a score out of ten, as in normal gymnastic competition, but try to beat their opponent. Teams should alternate performers. After the first girl in each team has performed, the student judge awards a point to the girl who did the best. The next two girls then compete and a point is awarded to the best performer. After all team members have competed in this way, a team score can be determined for that event.

If the official is efficient and competitors are ready when it is their turn, two squads of four or five members each can complete competition in one event in just a few minutes.

INTRAMURAL COMPETITION

Intramural competition can be either the dual meet or tournament type. There is no need to include a special intramural section in this book as the steps listed in this chapter, for either of these forms of competition can be followed in conducting competition within a school. Many of the items can be bypassed, however, in organizing an intramural meet. Judging and team scoring can be modified in a number of ways. It is certainly not necessary to have five judges as specified by the rules. Intramural meets can be judged and scored in the same way as described under item number ten in the previous section "Competition in Physical Education Classes."

PLANNING GYMNASTIC TOURNAMENTS

In a gymnastic tournament any number of teams or unattached individual competitors can compete. Careful planning is necessary to have a successful meet. This is also true for a swimming or track meet. It is no more difficult to run a gymnastic tournament than a meet in some other sport.

The following steps in planning for a meet are presented as a guide. This list includes all the steps necessary for a large championship meet in which many teams and competitors come from out

Lineup of Competitors During the Opening Ceremonies of the 1962 National A.A.U. Gymnastic Championships for Men and Women. The meet was held in the Seattle Arena on the World's Fair Grounds. Note the balance beam, men's parallel bars, trampoline, and floor exercise areas. Judges, score flashers, scorekeepers, and other officials are in position to start the first two events—the balance beam and the men's parallel bars.

of town. It is hoped that the length of the list is not frightening. Many items can be overlooked for an intramural meet or even an interschool meet with a limited number of participants from the local area.

STEPS IN PLANNING A GYMNASTIC TOURNAMENT

1. Form a games committee and select a meet director. An energetic teacher or coach can serve as a one-man games committee as well as the meet director if she wishes.
2. Select a date and time for the meet. Check to see that the date does not conflict with other activities.
3. Apply for a sanction from the local A.A.U. office if the meet is an open meet. This is not necessary if competitors are limited to those attending school and the meet is held in one of the participating schools.

4. Establish rules for the meet. It is always wise to make known to all coaches and competitors that unless otherwise stated the official rules of the A.A.U. or D.G.W.S. will govern the meet. The latest rule book should be used. In case a question or protest arises the meet director can then refer to the official source. For almost every meet there are rules that have to be modified and special regulations that have to be established, such as:

a. Who is eligible to compete?

b. How many levels of competition are to be held? Will everyone compete together or will they be divided by ability (beginners, intermediates, and advanced) or by school grades?

c. What events will be held? Is the all-round event to be included? Because of lack of equipment or lack of performers certain events are sometimes not held.

d. Are required, or optional, or both required and optional exercises to be used? (See item seven for further information.)

e. Will it be a single-session or two-session meet? What will be the order of events and time schedule of events?

f. How many girls may enter from each team? How many from one team may enter each event? The A.A.U. rules do not limit the number on a team or the number in an event from a single team.

g. How many events may an individual enter? The A.A.U. rules do not limit this but the rules of the D.G.W.S., which will be available in the near future, will limit the number of events.

h. How many places are to be scored and how will team points be awarded?

i. Are awards to be presented? If so, they should be ordered well in advance. Awards should be inexpensive and of the symbolic type.

j. Is an entry fee to be charged? It has become customary to charge a small entry fee for most meets to cover the cost of awards and incidental expenses. An entry fee usually insures that the competitor will actually show up for competition. A knowledge of the number of participants facilitates planning and organization.

k. Is there to be an entry deadline? A deadline at least a day before the meet enables the meet director to make last minute plans, to draw for order of competition, and to prepare score sheets in advance.

5. Appoint committees. If the meet is small this is not necessary, as the meet director can, and often does, handle all details herself. For a large meet, committees are usually established for several or all of the following: publicity, financing, equipment, housing of competitors, awards, duplication of results, program, first aid, judges, scorekeepers, score flashers, marshalls, and ushers.

6. Distribute the information bulletin and entry blanks to prospective competitors and coaches. This should be mailed to other schools or organizations several weeks in advance. For an intramural meet, posting pertinent information and a signup sheet on bulletin boards might be all that is necessary. Two example information bulletins and two example entry blanks are included in the appendix, pages 251–54. One of these, in each case, is suitable for an intramural meet, the others for a larger meet.

7. Distribute required exercises. If required exercises are to be used, they should be made available several weeks in advance. Usually exercises for large championship meets are available several months, or even as much as a year, in advance. These should be mailed out with an announcement of the coming meet, or if they are for an intramural meet they should be posted on the bulletin board in the gymnasium. Required exercises should always be tried out before adopting them. Usually revisions are necessary, as a routine that looks good on paper is not always practical. Advantages of required exercises are:

   a. They provide an example for the gymnast. This is especially valuable for a beginning gymnast.

   b. They set a standard for the meet. Students unable to learn the required exercises are eliminated.

   c. They stimulate interest by providing a goal.

   d. They are disciplinary in nature as competitors are forced to learn new skills or perform old skills in a particular way. Even the advanced gymnast is often forced to learn a skill that she has neglected.

   e. They are easier to judge than optional exercises because difficulty and technical value do not have to be considered.

   The main disadvantage of required exercises is that they force competitors to follow a pattern and allow no place for initiative, originality, and the presentation of the gymnasts' best and most difficult skills. If time permits, a combination of the two types of exercises can be used. If time does not permit, required exercises are best for the inexperienced gymnast, while optional exercises are best for the experienced gymnast.

8. Publicize the meet by using the usual mediums in the school, in the entire community, or throughout a wider area depending on the nature of the meet.

9. Make arrangements to house competitors if necessary. Meets that involve overnight stays should ordinarily be avoided for school teams.

10. Invite local dignitaries such as the principal, superintendent, and community leaders.

11. Plan the awards ceremony. Awards can be presented after each event, at special times throughout the meet or at the end of the meet. Presenting awards periodically throughout the meet is

probably the best method. A victory stand should be used, but the awards ceremony should not be overly emphasized so that winning seems more important than the recreational and physiological values of participation.

12. Provide enough equipment for an adequate warmup for all events. A duplicate set of equipment in an adjacent gymnasium is desirable. A policy that is now generally being followed is to forbid warmups on the floor of competition after the meet starts. If a certain piece of equipment were not available prior to the meet, an exception is made to this policy. Gymnasts should be instructed to be on the gym floor at least a half hour before the meet in order to warm up for all events.

13. Arrange for locker and shower facilities, provide towels and a checking service for valuables for visiting gymnasts.

14. Arrange for the necessary number of officials and other workers.

    a. Judges—The rules call for five scoring judges, a superior judge, and an extra judge to time or count in certain events. For a small meet this number can be reduced without affecting the success of the meet. For a large meet in which more than one event is held at a time a second set of judges has to be provided. A briefing or instructional session for judges prior to the meet is desirable.

    b. Scorekeepers—It is wise to have two scorekeepers who work independently and then check to see if they have obtained the same results. In this way mistakes are almost eliminated. If more than one event is held at a time, a second set of scorekeepers has to be provided. If an all-round score or team score is being kept, a separate scorekeeper should be assigned to these tasks. For a large meet a head scorekeeper should be appointed to coordinate the work and collect and safeguard all score sheets. Example score sheets are included in the Appendix, pages 255–58.

    c. Announcers—If only one event is held at a time, one announcer can handle a meet very satisfactorily. A public address system should be used for opening remarks, announcing each event, presentation of awards, calling competitors for competition, reading judges scores, and any special announcements. If two events are held at a time, two announcers are usually used, although one experienced announcer can handle the work.

    d. Score flashers—The work of the judges is made easier if each judge is provided with an assistant to flash her score to the scorekeepers. Flash cards can be made easily out of paper or cloth. Two pads with numbers from 1 to 10 tacked side by side on a piece of plywood enable the score flasher to flash any number from .1 to 10.0. Another common method of flashing scores is to use small slates and chalk. Another less common method is to have a clerk collect the judge's score on a slip of paper and take it to the scorekeepers.

e. Equipment men—There is always a certain amount of equipment moving or adjusting necessary just prior to, during, and after a meet. Depending on the size of the meet a crew of two to six individuals, who are familiar with the equipment, is needed.

f. Medical attendant—A doctor, nurse, or person qualified in first-aid is a desirable official to have on call for any athletic contest. The common first-aid materials should be available.

g. Pushers—"Pusher" is the name given to an individual who moves among the competitors and alerts them as their turn to compete approaches. These officials greatly speed up a meet by seeing that gymnasts are ready with sweat clothing off, hand guards on, and chalk applied.

h. Marshals—As in track and field, keeping the field of competition clear of unauthorized individuals is a problem. Marshals should be provided with an arm band or badge to identify them.

i. Other personnel—Ushers, program distributors, locker room attendants, etc., might be necessary for some meets.

15. Decide on event order and the number of events to be held at a time. This should be done well ahead of time, if possible, so that the information can be released in the information bulletin. Sometimes this cannot be done until the number of entries is known. If the information has not been released previously, or included in the program, it should be posted in several places for the benefit of competitors.

16. Diagram the placement of equipment on the floor and plan for the movement of equipment during the meet. Be sure to measure and mark the floor exercise area prior to the meet.

17. Have programs printed. The program should be planned and outlined well in advance. It is desirable to leave the actual printing of the program as late as possible in order to include information that is usually not available until just before the meet. Some of the usual items included in a gymnastic program are: the meet committee; officials; acknowledgments; time schedule of events; list of competitors with their numbers and team affiliation; order of competition for each event; informative information such as how gymnasts are judged, digest of rules, and how exercises are composed in each event; and a blank score sheet so that spectators can keep score.

18. Prepare score sheets. As soon as the entry deadline has passed, the order of competition can be drawn and score sheets prepared. It is desirable to have this information in the program, but if this is not possible the order of competition should be posted in several places so competitors can refer to it. It is desirable, but not

essential, that each judge have an order of competition list on which to write and record her score (see example scoresheet, Appendix pages 255–58).

19. Provide the following list of equipment besides the necessary gymnastic equipment: public address system; gymnastic chalk and resin for hands and feet; dry towels to wipe off equipment; wet towels for competitors feet; competitors' numbers; fine sandpaper to rub caked chalk off the beam and uneven bars; record player and tape recorder for competitors' floor exercise music; stop watch to time floor exercises, beam, tumbling, and the rest period on the trampoline; wrenches and tape measure to use in adjusting equipment; pencils, scratch pads, and clip boards for judges and scorekeepers; flash cards or slates, chalk, and erasers; chairs for judges, score flashers, and scorekeepers; tables for the superior judge and scorekeepers for each event; a table for the head scorekeeper (isolated from all the hustle and bustle of the meet); the awards and an award platform.

20. Provide for an adequate rest area, away from the competition for competitors.

21. Have results duplicated. In recent years it has been common practice to provide copies of the results for newspapers, coaches, and competitors. With a little planning this can be done within a few minutes after each event is over. There are a number of methods that can be used. If only a few copies are needed, the scorekeepers can keep carbon copies of their work. If more copies are needed, as each event is concluded the results can be quickly typed on a ditto sheet. A more efficient method to use, if many copies of the results are needed, is to prepare the ditto masters ahead of time. A few blank copies can then be run off in advance so judges can have these on which to work, so some can be posted for competitors, and so the scorekeepers can use these as work sheets. It is possible for the scorekeepers to keep score on the ditto master so that immediately upon conclusion of the event the results can be duplicated. The disadvantage of this method is the possibility of the scorekeepers making errors on the ditto master. For this reason it is best for them to keep score on work sheets and then quickly transfer the results to the ditto master after their work has been checked.

PLANNING DUAL GYMNASTIC MEETS

(NOTE: The suggestions below also apply to triangular or quadrangular meets.)

Dual meets are very easy to plan and conduct in comparison with the gymnastic tournament. All competitors are under the supervision of the two coaches. If the visiting team is from another school, the coach makes her own travel and housing arrangements. Dual meets are practically always one-session meets with one event held at a time so that only one set of officials is needed. There are usually no awards and no entry fees. There is no need to mail out information sheets or entry blanks. A letter or phone call to the opposing coach to establish procedures and regulations is all that is necessary.

STEPS IN PLANNING A DUAL MEET

1. Select a date and time for the meet. Avoid conflicts if possible. Arrange for use of facilities.
2. Select a meet director. The host coach almost always serves as meet director.
3. Establish rules for the meet. Some decision will have to be made by the two coaches regarding most of the items listed under number 4 in the previous section "Planning Gymnastic Tournaments." It is wise to agree that unless otherwise decided the latest rules of the D.G.W.S. or A.A.U. will apply. The only set of rules available in this country for dual meet competition is the National Collegiate Athletic Association Rules for men. These rules could be used as a pattern for such things as order of competition and team entry limit that are not a part of the A.A.U. or D.G.W.S. rules. The International Gymnastic Federation (F.I.G.) does have a set of women's dual meet rules used for international competition, but these do not include the tumbling and trampoline events and, moreover, they are not available at this time in the English language. In dual meets there is usually just one level of competition with three competitors from each team in each event. Teams alternate competitors in each event and in being "first-up" in each event. Required exercises are usually not used in dual meets, but there is no reason why they could not be used. It has been recommended previously that required exercises are desirable for inexperienced gymnasts.
4. Publicize the meet.
5. Invite school administrative personnel.
6. Provide for warmups prior to the meet. Warmups are usually not permitted on the floor after a dual meet has started.
7. Provide locker room facilities for the visiting team.
8. Arrange for the required number of officials and other workers. All of the same officials, in reduced numbers, are needed for a dual meet as an invitational tournament (except pushers). Refer to number 15 under "Planning Gymnastic Tournaments."
9. Diagram placement of equipment on the floor and plan for the movement of equipment during the meet. Be sure to measure and mark the floor exercise area before the meet.

10. Have programs printed. If the opposing team's entries can be obtained in advance for each event, this adds to the usefulness of the program.
11. Prepare score sheets. These should be prepared in advance with the host teams entries included. The visiting coach can make her entries just prior to the meet as the competitors are warming up. Example score sheets are included in the Appendix, pages 255–58.
12. Have necessary equipment, other than meet apparatus, available. This list is the same as for "Gymnastic Tournaments" except that competitors numbers, awards, and the award platform are not needed.
13. Provide a copy of the results for the visiting coach. Results do not have to be duplicated. If two scorekeepers are used, as mentioned previously, and each scorekeeper keeps a carbon copy of her work, there will be a set of results available for each coach plus two extra copies for newspapers.

CONDUCT OF A GYMNASTIC MEET

1. Announcer asks for warmups to cease and floor to be cleared.
2. Equipment men make any necessary shift of equipment.
3. Officials take their places ready for the first event. Judges usually place themselves around the piece of equipment as shown in the diagram. An alternate method is to have the judges in one straight line, slightly apart, along one side of the equipment.

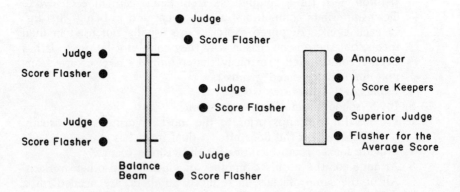

4. Announcer welcomes spectators and contestants, introduces judges, and makes any other necessary preliminary remarks.
5. Announcer calls the first competitor "up" and alerts the next two competitors by using the terms "on deck" and "in the hole."

6. The first competitor performs and is scored by the judges. The judges usually confer after the first competitor in each event but score all other competitors independently and without consultation. Judges reveal their score to their flasher.

7. Announcer asks for "scores" and the score flashers hold up scores simultaneously. The announcer then reads the scores for the spectators' benefit. The scorekeepers copy the scores visually (e.g., they don't rely on the reading of the scores by the announcer as mistakes might thus be made) and then compute the average score. The superior judge checks the scores to see that they are within the required range, computes the average, and has her score flasher hold up the average score as soon as it is available. The superior judge's average can serve as a double check by the scorekeepers.

8. Announcer then calls up the gymnast who has been "on deck" and alerts the next two girls. This procedure is followed until all contestants have performed in an event.

9. The next event is started and conducted in a similar manner. A good announcer will keep the audience informed by reporting results of the previous event promptly, explaining briefly the rules of each event, and naming some of the more spectacular stunts performed.

ORGANIZING TEAM PRACTICE SESSIONS

There are hundreds of girls' exhibition teams and gymnastic clubs in the schools across our country but very few competitive teams. The suggestions made here apply especially to practice sessions for competitive teams. It is hoped that with the tremendous upsurge in girls' gymnastics, in a few years there will be many more competitive teams with active coaches.

Until recently most coaches of men's teams have not held organized practice sessions. A team workout usually consisted of an informal period with team members wandering from one event to another. The coach, and maybe some of the better performers, would help first here, and then there, in a haphazard fashion. Gymnastic coaches have recently adopted the methods of coaches of other sports who are forced to get the most out of their players in order to compete successfully. The way to develop top teams in gymnastics is to have organized, scientifically planned practice sessions just as there are in other sports.

Practice sessions should be planned for a week at a time. Each week prior to the start of the season of competition is organized in much the same way. Once competition starts a new weekly plan is put into effect and this remains somewhat standard throughout the season.

Gymnasts can be divided into two groups—the all-round performers and the specialists. The largest group of specialists in girls gymnastics is the group that specializes in trampoline and tumbling. Girls seldom specialize in one of the all-round events. If a girl does specialize in one event she can devote her whole time to the practice of this event, working with a group part of the time and on her own part of the time. Those who combine tumbling and trampoline as a specialty can divide their time between these two events each workout session.

As most female gymnasts today want to become all-round performers, practice sessions are usually planned with this in mind. The all-round performers should be assigned to a piece of equipment with girls of their own ability for a specified length of time. A variation of this might be when one or two advanced girls are assigned to help with groups of lesser ability during some practice sessions. At the end of the time limit groups shift to another piece of equipment and work on that for a specified period of time. If considerable time is available, the all-round performers cover all events each day; if less time is available, they work two events one day and the other two the next day.

The daily schedule can follow a number of patterns. Some examples of these are shown at right.

	Mon.	Tues.	Wed.	Thurs.	Fri.
I. Preseason	Learn new stunts	Practice required exercises—all events	Learn new stunts	Practice optional exercises—all-events	Learn new stunts
II. Preseason	Learn new stunts	Practice routines—two events	Learn new stunts	Practice routines—the other two events	Demonstration of complete required and optional routines in all events.
III. During season	Practice routines, all events	Work on weak events, on new stunts from all events, on new stunts needed badly to add to present routines	Demonstration of complete required and optional routines	Free day, not too much work, work favorite event or the event that needs the most work.	Competition in all events, either with another team or within ones own team.
IV. During season	Practice two events (routines chiefly)	Practice the other two events (routines chiefly)	Demonstration of complete routines, all events	Complete rest, do not report to gym	Competition in all events, either with another team or within one's own team.

249

Appendix

University of Washington
Intramural Gymnastics
INFORMATION BULLETIN

GENERAL INFORMATION

1. Teams may enter as many girls as they wish in the qualifying meet.
2. There will be required exercises for the qualifying meet. These are available in the intramural office.
3. Optional exercises only in the final meet.
4. The eight top performers in each event in the qualifying meet will advance into the final meet.
5. Contestants may enter a maximum of four events plus the all-round.
6. Unless otherwise stated, the Official Rules of the A.A.U. of the U.S. will apply. Copies are on reserve in the physical education office.
7. The team championship shall be awarded to the organization scoring the highest number of points in the final meet. There must be at least two contestants scoring points for a team. Points shall be scored as follows: 7 points for first, 5 for second, 4 for third, 3 for fourth, 2 for fifth, and 1 for sixth place.

EVENTS

1. Balance Beam
2. Side Horse Vault
3. Uneven Parallel Bars
4. Floor Exercises
5. Tumbling
6. Trampoline
7. All-Round—The all-round championship will be awarded to the individual obtaining the highest total score in the final meet in events 1 through 4.

COACHING

Coaching will be available at the following times starting January 4.
Monday, Tuesday, Thursday, and Friday   4:00–5:30 P.M.
Wednesday   7:30–9:30 P.M.

ENTRIES MUST BE IN THE INTRAMURAL OFFICE BY MONDAY, FEBRUARY 20

Those wishing to participate must indicate the events they wish to enter on individual entry blanks by February 20th.

251

QUALIFYING MEET—WEDNESDAY, FEBRUARY 22, 7:00 P.M.,
MAIN GYM

The first eight places in each event will be eligible for the final meet.

FINAL MEET—WEDNESDAY, MARCH 8, 7:00 P.M., MAIN GYM

INFORMATION BULLETIN

1962 Pacific Northwest A.A.U. Gymnastic Championship
Friday and Saturday March 17 and 18, 1962
Bellevue Senior High School

RULES AND REGULATIONS

1. The rules governing this meet will be the 1961 official rules of the A.A.U. of the United States.
2. Competitors can not compete in the same event in two divisions. The exception to this would be a competitor forced into a higher class because he has won the event in the division below, but who is still competing in the all-round in the lower division.
3. The entry fee for novice men, junior men, novice women, and junior women is $1.00; senior men and women $2.00. Fees must accompany entries.
4. No entries will be accepted after 5:00 P.M. Monday, March 13. Entries will not be accepted unless accompanied by entry fee.
5. Gymnasts from outside the Pacific Northwest Association of the A.A.U. must furnish travel permits.
6. Time Schedule:

Women		Men	
Novice		Novice	
Compulsory	9:00 A.M. Sat.	Compulsory	9:00 A.M. Sat.
Optional	2:00 P.M. Sat.	Optional	2:00 P.M. Sat.
Junior		Junior	
Compulsory	9:00 A.M. Sat.	Compulsory	9:00 A.M. Sat.
Optional	2.00 P.M. Sat.	Optional	2:00 P.M. Sat.
Senior		Senior	
Compulsory	7:30 P.M. Fri.	Compulsory	7:30 P.M. Fri.
Optional	7:30 P.M. Sat.	Optional	7:30 P.M. Sat.

GENERAL INFORMATION

1. Nissen-Medart equipment meeting all F.I.G. requirements will be used. A floor exercise pad, 60-foot tumbling mat, and Goliath trampolines will be available.
2. A map giving directions to Bellevue High School is enclosed.

3. Those wishing to be billeted with a Bellevue family should fill out the enclosed form and return it immediately.
4. A copy of the required exercises is enclosed. Others can be obtained on request.
5. The Bellevue High School gym will be available for practice on Wednesday and Thursday evenings from 7:30 to 9:30 for those who arrive early.
6. Regulation A.A.U. Championship Medals will be awarded to the first three place winners in each event. Ribbons will be awarded to 4th, 5th, and 6th place.
7. Contestants and coaches should report to the contestants' table in the gym lobby to pick up their official envelope containing their numbers, gate passes, programs, and other general information. Travel permits must be presented at this time.
8. Please send publicity releases with photos as soon as possible to the meet director.
9. Meals will be provided, for a small charge, in the school cafeteria on Friday evening, Saturday noon, and Saturday evening.
10. Meetings—Judges—Gym, Friday 4:00 P.M.
    Technical Committee—Gym, Friday 6:00 P.M.
    Coaches and Pacific Northwest Gymnastic Committee—Cafeteria, Saturday 12:00 Noon; Lunch will be served.
11. Additional information may be obtained by writing to the Meet Director: Miss Nancy Banks, Bellevue Senior High School, Bellevue, Wash.

UNIVERSITY OF WASHINGTON
DEPARTMENT OF INTRAMURAL SPORTS

GYMNASTIC ENTRY BLANK

Date _____ 19_____

I wish to enter the following events (check):

Floor Exercises _____ Tumbling _____

Balance Beam _____ Trampoline _____

Side Horse Vault _____ All-Round _____

Uneven Parallel Bars _____

Name _____ Address _____

Home Phone _____ Organization _____

1962
Pacific Northwest A.A.U. Gymnastic Championship

OFFICIAL ENTRY BLANK

Entries close Monday, March 13, 1962

Events for Men

Events	Novice	Junior	Senior
Floor Exercise			
Side Horse			
Long Horse			
Horizontal Bar			
Parallel Bars			
Still Rings			
All-Round			
Tumbling			
Trampoline			
Rope Climb			
Flying Rings			

Events for Women

Events	Novice	Junior	Senior
Floor Exercise			
Balance Beam			
Side Horse Vault			
Uneven Parallel Bars			
All-Round			
Tumbling			
Trampoline			

Place an X opposite the events you wish to enter and in the division in which you wish to participate.

Novice men, junior men, novice women, and junior women $1.00. Senior men and women $2.00.

Entry fees must accompany entry blanks.

Release: I hereby for myself, my heirs, and executors waive and release any and all rights and claims for damages that I may have at any time against the A.A.U., or Bellevue High School, or their agents and representatives, for any injuries or damages that may be suffered by me in connection with my association, or entry in, the above meet at Bellevue High School, March 17 and 18, 1962.

Signature _____

If contestant is under 21 years of age
Signature of Parent or Guardian _____

Please Print

Contestant's Name _____ Age _____
Street Address _____ City _____
Team Affiliation _____ A.A.U. Card No. _____

Meet information may be obtained by writing to the Meet Director:
Miss Nancy Banks, Bellevue Senior High School, Bellevue, Washington

GYMNASTIC SCORE SHEET
WOMEN'S SPECIAL EVENTS

MEET _____ JUDGES 1 _____

LOCATION _____ 2 _____

DATE _____ 3 _____

4 _____

EVENT _____ 5 _____

Superior _____

COMP. NUMBER	NAME	TEAM AFFIL.	1	2	3	4	5	TOTAL	AVE.	PLACE	TEAM SCORE

GYMNASTIC SCORE SHEET
WOMEN'S ALL-ROUND EVENTS

MEET_____ JUDGES 1 _____

LOCATION _____ 2 _____

DATE _____ 3 _____

4 _____

EVENT _____ 5 _____

Superior _____

COMP. NUMBER	NAME	TEAM AFFIL.	EXER-CISE	JUDGES 1	2	3	4	5	TOTAL	AVE.	GRAND TOTAL	PLACE	TEAM SCORE
			COMP.										
			OPT.										
			COMP.										
			OPT.										
			COMP.										
			OPT.										
			COMP.										
			OPT.										
			COMP.										
			OPT.										
			COMP.										
			OPT.										
			COMP.										
			OPT.										
			COMP.										
			OPT.										
			COMP.										
			OPT.										
			COMP.										
			OPT.										
			COMP.										
			OPT.										
			COMP.										
			OPT.										
			COMP.										
			OPT.										
			COMP.										
			OPT.										
			COMP.										
			OPT.										

GYMNASTICS SCORE SHEET
WOMEN'S ALL-ROUND EVENT

MEET _____ LOCATION _____ DATE _____

EVENTS										
NAME										
AFFILIATION										
BALANCE BEAM	Event Score									
	Running Score									
SIDE HORSE VAULT	Event Score									
	Running Score									
UNEVEN PARALLEL BARS	Event Score									
	Running Score									
FLOOR EXERCISES	Event Score									
	Running Score									
TOTAL SCORE										
PLACE										
TEAM SCORE										

WOMEN'S GYMNASTICS
TEAM SCORING FORM

MEET_____

LOCATION_____ DATE_____

EVENTS						
BALANCE BEAM	Event Score					
	Running Score					
SIDE HORSE VAULT	Event Score					
	Running Score					
UNEVEN PARALLELS	Event Score					
	Running Score					
FLOOR EXERCISES	Event Score					
	Running Score					
ALL-ROUND	Event Score					
	Running Score					
TUMBLING	Event Score					
	Running Score					
TRAMPOLINE	Event Score					
	Running Score					
FINAL SCORE						
PLACE						

Glossary

A.A.H.P.E.R.—American Association for Health, Physical Education and Recreation.

A.A.U.—Amateur Athletic Union of the United States.

ALL-ROUND (WOMEN)—An event in which the winner is determined by totaling the scores received in the following four events: balance beam, floor exercises, side horse vaulting, and uneven parallel bars.

ARABESQUE—A one-leg balance in which the other leg is raised backward to a horizontal position while the trunk remains almost vertical.

ARCH (LAYOUT, HOLLOW BACK)—A position in which the body is curved, like an arc of a circle, with the hips forward and the upper trunk and legs extended backward.

BACKWARD—A direction of movement in which the back of the head and back lead the movement (there are a few exceptions.)

BARONI (BRANI, BRANDY)—A name given to a special type of a half-twisting front somersault with the body in a pike position.

BEAT BOARD—A short inclined board used for mounting the balance beam and uneven parallel bars.

BED OF THE TRAMPOLINE—A term used to refer to the woven nylon or canvas surface of the trampoline on which the performer bounces.

BREADTH AXIS—An imaginary line drawn laterally through the body from shoulder to shoulder.

BREAK—A point in an exercise at which a gymnast makes a mistake or has an unintentional pause.

CAST—A term used to describe movements in which the body is first piked and then extended upward and away from the point of grasp in either a forward or backward direction.

CENTER OF GRAVITY—The center of the distribution of body weight. The point of balance.

CHASSE—A dance step in which a slide on one foot is followed closely and in a gallop-like rhythm by a slide on the other.

CIRCLE—A movement in which the body (or sometimes a part of the body, such as the legs) travels completely around a point of support.

CODY—A name given to a backward somersault on the trampoline executed from a front drop landing.

COMPULSORY EXERCISE (PRESCRIBED EXERCISE, REQUIRED EXERCISE)—The term used to refer to a competitive gymnastic exercise which every competitor must perform.

CONTINUITY—A term used to refer to the smoothness or flowing quality of a routine or series. A series is said to possess continuity if it is not interrupted by undesirable pauses, stops, or extra movements.

259

CROSS—A position in which the breadth axis of the performer is perpendicular to the long axis of the apparatus.

CUT—A movement in which one or both legs swing between the hand or hands and a piece of equipment. In a cut-on the performer starts on the floor and ends on the equipment. In a cut-off the performer dismounts during the cut.

D.G.W.S.—Division for Girls and Women's Sports of the American Association for Health, Physical Education and Recreation.

DISLOCATE—A movement in which the body, while suspended from a fixed point by the hands, makes a complete circle or revolution, rotating around the shoulder joint, in a backward direction.

DISMOUNT—A stunt used by the performer to get off the apparatus. In a competitive exercise a dismount is the last stunt, or short series of stunts in the exercise. The last series of a floor exercise routine is sometimes referred to as the dismount.

EXERCISE (ROUTINE)—A planned continuous series of stunts that a gymnast performs in competition in every event except vaulting.

F.I.G.—International Gymnastic Federation. This organization governs and makes rules for international competition.

FLANK—A term used to describe a movement, stunt, or position in which the side of the body is toward the apparatus.

FLIP—A common term for somersault.

FORWARD—A direction of movement in which the face or chest leads the movement.

FRONT (FRONTWAYS)—Two terms used to describe a movement, stunt, or position in which the front of the body is facing the apparatus.

GOLIATH TRAMPOLINE (JUMBO)—Two terms used for a trampoline that is larger than the usual size used in schools (common frame size—9′ × 15′; goliath frame size—10′ × 17′.)

GRIP (GRASP)—Two terms that refer to the handhold that the gymnast has on the apparatus. Many different grips are used.

> *Regular* (*ordinary, over, front*)—when the palms face in the opposite direction from the body in a support position or in the same direction as the body in a hang.
>
> *Reverse* (*under*)—when the palms of the hands face in the same direction as the body in a support position and in the opposite direction from the body in the hang.
>
> *Cross*—when the arms are crossed so that the left hand is at the right of the right hand.
>
> *Mixed* (*combined*)—when one hand is in a reverse grip and the other hand in a regular grip.
>
> *Rotated*—a reverse grasp in which the hands have been turned 360 degrees from the normal reverse grip.

HANG—A position in which the center of gravity, and usually the entire body, is below the point of support. The point of support is usually the hands but is sometimes the knees, the feet, the elbows, or the arms.

HOP—A spring into the air with a takeoff from one foot and a landing on the same foot.

INTERNATIONAL EVENTS (OLYMPIC)—The events used officially in all international gymnastic competition, including the Olympic games. The four international women's events are—the balance beam, floor exercises, the side horse vault, and the uneven parallel bars.

JUMP—A spring into the air with a takeoff from both feet.

KILLING THE BOUNCE—A term used when the bounce on the trampoline is suddenly stopped so that the feet remain in contact with the bed. It is accomplished by flexing the knees rapidly as the feet contact the bed.

KIP—A movement from a hang to a support in which the body pikes and then rapidly extends.

"L"—A position in which the legs are forward in a horizontal plane so that they form a right angle with the trunk. The correct term is a half-lever.

LEAP—A spring into the air, taking off from one foot and landing on the other.

LEVER—A position in which the body is held horizontal to the floor. If the legs only are horizontal, the position is called a half-lever.

LONGITUDINAL AXIS—An imaginary line running from the top of the head through the center of the body to the soles of the feet.

LUNGE—A standing position in which the legs are apart with one knee bent and the other straight. This term also refers to the "movement" from a vertical standing position to the position described.

MOUNT—A stunt used by the performer to get on the apparatus. In a competitive exercise it is the first stunt or short series of stunts in a balance beam or uneven bar routine. The first series in floor exercises is sometimes referred to as a mount.

N.C.A.A.—National Collegiate Athletic Association. This is one of the organizations that controls men's intercollegiate athletics.

OFFSETS—The uneven parallel bars.

OPTIONAL EXERCISE (VOLUNTARY EXERCISE)—The term used to refer to a competitive gymnastic exercise which is composed by the individual from stunts of her own choice.

PIKE—A position in which the body is flexed at the waist with the legs straight. In most pike positions the trunk and legs form approximately a right angle. It is called an open pike if the legs are only slightly flexed and a tight pike if the legs are considerably flexed.

PIROUETTE—A movement around the longitudinal axis of the body with the body in a vertical position, either upright or inverted, throughout the turn.

PIVOT—A smooth turn left or right on the balls of one or both feet.

PRESS—A movement into a head or hand balance that involves a shifting of body weight and a slow, steady muscular action rather than a kick up or a swing up.

REAR (REARWAYS)—Two terms used to describe a movement, stunt, or position in which the rear of the body is toward the apparatus.

REBOUND TUMBLING—A term used for stunts done on the trampoline.

REUTHER BOARD—The official takeoff board used in vaulting and sometimes other gymnastic events. The reuther board was developed in Germany and is of very recent origin.

ROLL—A circling movement in which the body remains in contact with, and the body weight is supported by, the mat or equipment during the entire movement. The back is usually rounded and the legs tucked or piked during the roll.

ROUTINE (EXERCISE)—A planned continuous series of stunts performed in every event in gymnastic competition except vaulting.

SCALE—A one-leg balance in which the other leg is raised backward and the trunk lowered forward to a position approximately horizontal to the floor.

SEAT—A position in which most of the weight is supported by the thighs or buttocks. Seats are usually described according to the relationship of the body to the apparatus. Examples—cross seat, straddle seat, side seat, inner or outer seats.

SIDE—A position in which the breadth axis of the gymnast is parallel to the long axis of the apparatus. This is a rather confusing term as it has no connection to the side of the body. The gymnast faces toward or away from the equipment in a side position.

SISSONE—A jump into the air from both feet with the left foot turned out to the side and the right foot held perpendicular to the left foot with the heel against the instep of the left foot. The feet change position in the air so that the landing is on both feet with the position of the feet reversed.

SOMERSAULT (SOMI, FLIP)—A complete circling motion of the body in the air, usually from feet to feet, during which no other part of the body comes in contact with the mat or apparatus.

SPECIAL EVENTS—A term used to classify the tumbling and trampoline events, the two women's gymnastic events that are not all-round or international events.

SPLIT—A position in which both legs are held straight and at right angles to the trunk. Usually one leg is directly forward and one directly backward.

SPOTTING—The term used to refer to the proper positioning of an individual who assists a gymnast in the performance of a stunt. Spotting is also commonly used to refer to the actual "act of assisting" and the person providing the assistance is called the "spotter."

SPRING—A complete circling motion of the body in the air, usually from feet to feet, in which the hands, head, neck, or shoulders contact the mat or apparatus during the movement.

STAND—A position on the floor or apparatus in which the entire body is above the point of support. The point of support is usually the feet but can be the knees, hands, head, forearms, or shoulders.

STRADDLE—A position in which the legs are spread wide apart.

SUPPORT (REST)—A position in which the weight is supported wholly or partially by the hands with the shoulders above the point of grasp and the center of gravity below the shoulders.

SWING—A movement in which the body describes a circle, or an arc of a circle, while in a hang or support position.

SWING-UP—A smooth circling movement in which the gymnast changes from a hang to a support.

TOUR JETÉ—A leap off of one foot with a half turn in the air to a landing on the other foot.

TUCK—A position in which the head is forward with the chin close to the chest, the back is rounded, and the knees are drawn up to the chest.

TWIST—A turn left or right around one's longitudinal axis.

UPRISE—A movement from a hang to a support, at the end of a forward or backward swing, in which the head remains above the center of gravity.

VAULT—A jump or leap over a piece of apparatus in which one or both hands touch the apparatus during the movement.

Bibliography

Amateur Athletic Union of the United States. *1962–63 Official Guide,* New York 7, New York. 217 pages. This guide is published every two years. It contains the official rules for men and women; international, national, and district meet summaries; inspirational and informative reports and articles; and compulsory exercises for men and women.

Burns, Ted. *Tumbling Techniques Illustrated.* New York: The Ronald Press Company, 1957. 96 pages. This text is for both men and women. It includes single tumbling stunts for beginners, intermediates, and advanced performers.

Griswold, Larry. *Trampoline Tumbling.* St. Louis, Mo.: Business Collaborators Inc., 1958. 120 pages. This book has chapters on history, notes for instructors, body mechanics, fundamental bounces, basic exercises, simple demonstrations, advanced exercises, suggested routines, group tumbling, exhibitions, competition. It is illustrated with drawings.

Harris, Rich. *Physical Education and Rebound Tumbling.* Cedar Rapids, Iowa: Barnes Publishing Company, 1961. 48 pages. This pamphlet includes information on values, safety, equipment, class organization, basic instruction, lesson plans, and where to obtain reference materials. It is illustrated with photos and drawings.

———. *Saftey and Rebound Tumbling.* Cedar Rapids, Iowa: Barnes Publishing Company, 1960. 21 pages. This pamphlet contains chapters on safety in schools, safety in recreation, mechanics of safety, and rules for safety. It is illustrated with photographs.

Horn, Virginia Lee. *Stunts and Tumbling for Girls.* New York: The Ronald Press Company, 1943. 219 pages. This text contains information on single, double, and group tumbling stunts, balances, and pyramids. It is illustrated with stick figures and photographs.

Keeney, Chuck. *Trampolining Illustrated.* New York: The Ronald Press Company, 1961. 160 pages. Keeney presents fifty trampoline stunts ranging from the simplest to the most difficult. The book is illustrated with photos.

Kunzle, G. C. *Horizontal Bar.* London: James Barrie Books, Ltd., 1957. 269 pages. This text is devoted entirely to the men's horizontal bar event. Dozens of stunts that are very usable on the uneven parallel bars are described in detail. Spotting techniques as well as the stunts themselves are illustrated with photographs.

LaDue, Frank, and Norman, Jim. *Two Seconds of Freedom.* Cedar Rapids, Iowa: Nissen Trampoline Company, 1960. 167 pages. This text explains and illustrates with photographs a great number of trampoline stunts from beginning to advanced.

Lienert, Walter. *The Modern Girl Gymnast on the Uneven Parallel Bars.* Indianapolis, Indiana, 1957. 56 pages. This text is the most complete source available for the uneven parallel bar event. Stunts ranging from beginning to advanced are explained and illustrated with drawings.

Loken, Newton C. (How to Improve series). *Beginning Tumbling and Balancing* 1951; *Advanced Tumbling and Balancing* 1958; *Trampolining* 1958; *Gymnastics for Girls and Women* 1958. The Athletic Institute, Chicago, Ill. These are very small pamphlets. The title of each indicates the content. They are illustrated with photographs.

――――. *Complete Book of Gymnastics.* Englewood Cliffs, N.J.: Prentice-Hall, Inc.,
1959. 212 pages. This text has a chapter on every men's and women's gymnastic
event as well as special activities such as balancing, calisthenics, women's even
parallel bars, rope, and springboard trampoline. It also has chapters on history,
values, and gymnastic exhibitions. Stunts are illustrated with photographs.

MacLEAN, DOROTHY. *Gymnastics Guide.* Washington, D.C.: Am. Asso. for Health,
Phys. Educ., & Recreation, 1963. 112 pages. This guide contains information
about the D.G.W.S. and its rules & standards for gymnastic competition. It also
contains many informative articles by a variety of well known authors.

McCLOW, L. L. *Tumbling Illustrated.* New York: The Ronald Press Company, 1931.
212 pages. This book explains and illustrates with stick figures a great number of
single, double, and group tumbling and balancing stunts. It is an excellent source
for those looking for many novelty stunts suitable for exhibitions as well as class
use.

The Modern Gymnast. Santa Monica, Calif. This is a magazine devoted entirely
to the sport of gymnastics and is published approximately every two months. It
contains many photographs, reports on meets and clinics, and informative articles
for both men and women. It also contains lists of sources for gymnastic films,
equipment, uniforms, and books.

MOSSCROP, ALFREDA and HARDENBERGH, HELEN. *Descriptive Analysis of Selected
Apparatus Events for Girls and Women* (1957 Printing). Minneapolis: Burgess
Publishing Company, 1931. 60 pages. This text is rather out of date but is one
of the few sources available for women's apparatus work. It contains chapters
on box horse, side horse vaulting, buck horse, even parallel bars, horizontal ladder,
boom, traveling rings, and ropes.

National Collegiate Athletic Association. *Boxing, Gymnastics and Skiing Rules 1961–
62.* Kansas City, Mo., 1961–62. 64 pages. This book contains the men's collegiate gymnastic rules and is published every two years by the N.C.A.A.

RUFF, WESLEY K. *Gymnastics, Beginner to Competitor.* Dubuque, Iowa: W. C.
Brown Company, 1959. 204 pages. This book is designed for men but contains
much material suitable for women in chapters on tumbling and balancing, trampoline, and horizontal bar.

SZYPULA, GEORGE. *Tumbling and Balancing for All.* Dubuque, Iowa: W. C. Brown
Company, 1957. 161 pages. This text is primarily designed for men, but most of
the stunts included can be performed by girls. It contains information on spotting, class conduct, as well as descriptions of single and double tumbling and
balancing stunts. There are also sections on advanced competitive tumbling
routines and officiating. It is illustrated with photographs.

TAKEMOTO, MASAO. *Illustrated Women's Gymnastics.* Tokyo, Japan: San-Yu Shup-
pan Company Ltd. 225 pages. (American supplier: Frank Endo, Los Angeles 44,
Calif.) This book is written in Japanese but it contains so many excellent photographs and drawings that it can be very valuable to those who cannot read
Japanese. It includes three events—balance beam, vaulting, and uneven parallel
bars.

YEAGER, PATRICK. *A Teacher's Guide for Women's Gymnastics.* Statesboro, Ga.:
Georgia Southern College, 1962. This book is an excellent source of material for
the four women's international events.

INDEX